Transforming Vision

Writers on Art

Selected and introduced by Edward Hirsch

The Art Institute of Chicago

A Bulfinch Press Book
Little, Brown and Company
Boston • New York • Toronto • London

The Art Institute of Chicago gratefully acknowledges the Woman's Board for
its support of this publication.

Susan F. Rossen, Executive Director of Publications
Carol Jentsch Rutan, Editor
Katherine Houck Fredrickson, Associate Director of Publications-Production
Manine Rosa Golden, Production Associate
Kristin Chambers, Editorial Assistant

All photography by the Department of Imaging and Technical Services,
Alan B. Newman, Executive Director, unless otherwise noted on p. 143.

Designed by Ed Marquand, Marquand Books, Inc., Seattle, Wash.
Typeset in Dante by Monotype at Marquand Books
Color separations by Professional Graphics, Rockford, Ill.
Printed by CS Graphics, Singapore

Front cover: Henri Matisse, *Woman Before an Aquarium,* 1921, p. 47.
Frontispiece: Edward Hopper, *Nighthawks* (detail), 1942, p. 65.

Library of Congress Cataloging-in-Publication Data
Transforming vision : writers on art / selected and introduced by Edward
    Hirsch.
       p.   cm.
    "A Bulfinch Press book."
    ISBN 0-8212-2126-4: $27.95
    1. American poetry—20th century. 2. Art—Poetry. 3. Art. I. Hirsch,
Edward. II. Art Institute of Chicago.
PS595.A75T73   1994
810.8'0357—dc20   94-17323
                                                    CIP

EDWARD HIRSCH

 ACKNOWLEDGMENTS

This book grew directly out of conversations I have had over
the past several years with many friends and colleagues at
The Art Institute of Chicago. Not long after attending a read-
ing I gave at the School of the Art Institute of my poems, some
of which are inspired by works of art, Susan F. Rossen, the
museum's Executive Director of Publications, approached me
about the possibility of participating in an anthology of literary
work based on the Art Institute's outstanding collections. James
N. Wood, Director and President, supported the project from
its earliest stages. Also critical were the impetus and encourage-
ment of Mary Sue Glosser, Senior Lecturer in the Department
of Education, who involved me in the marvelous Lannan Liter-
ary Series and had me lead several workshops in the galleries
on poetry and art for area high schools. I am grateful to the
staff of the Publications Department, most especially to Carol
Jentsch Rutan, as well as to Kathy Fredrickson, Manine Golden,
and Kristin Chambers, who steered the book across every
impasse; to Ed Marquand for its elegant design; and to Brian
Hotchkiss of Bulfinch Press, for his belief in the project. Spe-
cial thanks are due to the Department of Imaging and Tech-
nical Services, under Alan Newman, for helping to make the
book a visual reality. I am also deeply grateful to the Art
Institute's Woman's Board, and its chair, Marcia Wagner, for
critical assistance with funding. Thanks too go to my agent,
Liz Darhansoff. My greatest personal debt is to Janet Landay,
a curator at the Museum of Fine Arts, Houston, who is also
my wife. Finally the mind boggles at the thought of assem-
bling for a group portrait the astonishing array of writers and
artists who contributed to this collection. Only a Hogarth or
a Seurat could do justice to the subject.

CONTENTS

EDWARD HIRSCH

INTRODUCTION

Transforming Vision is a book of encounters and responses, of imaginative acts of attention. Here a group of poets and prose writers seek to "translate" visual into verbal emblems, to find linguistic correlatives for what they are seeing. Description often initiates this activity (and these writers bring a great deal of descriptive acuity to their projects) but is invariably transformed into interpretation, into a space where one work of art generates and interpolates another. These pieces are personal interventions and meditations, creative inquiries, acts of inheritance. They illuminate individual works in the nineteenth- and twentieth-century collections of The Art Institute of Chicago by imaginatively entering into them, by teasing out their origins and implications—charting their methods, situating them in history or in experience, creating parallel or analogous literary worlds. Embodiment is all. The process is akin to what Robert Frost called "counter-love, original response."

The Art Institute of Chicago has always seemed to me an unsurpassed urban splendor, a Beaux-Arts chunk of the sublime carved out of Indiana limestone. "It is not unlikely that the Chicago Art Institute, with its splendid collection of casts and pictures, has done more for the people of the Middle West than any of the city's great industries," Willa Cather wrote in 1895. Over the past century, a large number of writers have drifted along with everyone else through the light-filled galleries. The experience is indelible, and many have felt special affinities with a collection at once so suggestive, so surprising, and so diverse, both intimate and expansive, central, transfiguring. How well I remember my first solo trips to the museum in the mid-1960s: the nervous excitement of coming downtown on the El, the freedom of drifting through the crowds on State Street toward the open spaces of Lake Michigan, the scarcely concealed exaltation of rushing up the stairs between the tutelary bronze

lions. Like innumerable others, I countered my world by entering the Art Institute's imaginative precincts. I, too, have stood, awestruck and amazed, before Edward Hopper's vision of American loneliness, before Georges Seurat's monumental rendering of a bourgeois afternoon on the Seine. ("This is the celebration of contemplation," Delmore Schwartz once wrote, "This is the conversion of experience to pure attention.") What better place to engage the visual terms of modernity, to write one's fledgling poems (for me, it was literature for art's sake, and vice versa), to read Wallace Stevens's "Man with the Blue Guitar" in the shadow of Pablo Picasso's *Old Guitarist*. ("Is this picture of Picasso's, this 'hoard / Of destructions,' a picture of ourselves, / Now, an image of our society?" Stevens's poem asks.) Here the words gain strength from their blue light. Meditation in turn colors what we see. "One of the characteristic symptoms of the spiritual condition of our age," Charles Baudelaire said about Eugène Delacroix, is that "the arts aspire, if not to take one another's place, at least reciprocally to lend one another new powers."

· · ·

Transforming Vision begins with two personal encounters with the museum itself: a section of Willa Cather's "On Various Minor Painters" and of Stuart Dybek's book *The Coast of Chicago*. Nearly a century apart, these two appreciations capture a sense of the museum's persistent and unsettling magic, the urgency of being pulled back by certain talismanic paintings. Each subsequent piece then takes up and confronts an individual work in the collections. (For practical reasons we have limited ourselves to the past two centuries.) More than two-thirds of these writings are new; they were written expressly for this book. These have been supplemented by a number of other relevant examples—among them paragraphs from novels by Willa Cather and Saul Bellow; poems by Mina Loy, Carl Sandburg, Robert Hayden, and others; a sizable passage from Blaise Cendrars's memoir of Robert Delaunay, and so forth. Taken together, these fictions, poems, and personal essays constitute a richly varied set of responses to an equally varied set of prints and drawings, photographs, paintings, and sculptures.

This book began to come into focus last year when we invited a number of writers to respond to work in the permanent collections. We asked for short pieces in any form the writer deemed appropriate. It seemed better to avoid duplications, but the writers were otherwise left to their own devices to choose—to be chosen by—any work that intrigued them. The response was immediate and enthusiastic, unwavering. Feeling for the Art Institute runs high. Many asked for catalogues and photographs to jog and supplement their memories; others recalled with rapturous exactitude their many visits to the museum, their experiences with the art itself. It would seem the Art Institute was a secret each of us had discovered on his or her own. Many felt called upon to testify to what they had beheld.

I am responsible for the list of imaginative writers invited to participate. Their contributions have more than confirmed my high regard for their work. At the same time, however, space limitations have been rigorous and there are many marvelous poets and prose writers who have not been heard from this time around. I regret their absence, and I recognize that we could have made as fine a book with an entirely different cast of writers. I have also had to exclude a number of poems because they address well-known works otherwise represented—most notably, Frank O'Hara's "On Looking at *La Grande Jatte,* the Czar Wept Anew" and Ira Sadoff's prose poems "Seurat" and "Hopper's 'Nighthawks' (1942)." It would be possible to make a small, first-rate anthology consisting entirely of works that deal with Seurat's and Hopper's masterworks.

Not everyone we invited was able to participate. A few were puzzled by the ekphrastic mode; others were already committed to long-standing projects and deadlines. One writer, Sandra Cisneros, was so dispirited by the scarcity of Chicano artists represented that she simply listed the names of the only two Chicano photographers and wrote, "We're the only ones here." On the other hand, Philip Levine was so impelled by Lyonel Feininger's work that he wrote three fine poems about Feininger's paintings (we have been able to include only one of them). By and large, the writers we contacted responded to the project with a certain exaltation. They warmed to its conception, its process, and its premises, to the challenge of enacting their aesthetic reactions in equivalent works of their own devising.

Transforming Vision is not a guide to the collections, for many important artists are not represented. In the end, the writers spoke only to what spoke to them, to works that instigated their own voices. Their pieces are self-revealing, their registers personal. William Maxwell articulates the reigning spirit when he recalls, "The first time I saw the little Boudin beach scene, in the gallery devoted to nineteenth-century French painting, I cried out with pleasure."

• • •

I have been aware, in editing this collection, that there is always something transgressive in writing about the visual arts, in approaching the painter, the sculptor, or the photographer's work in words. A border is crossed, a boundary breached as the writer enters into the spatial realm, traducing an abyss, violating the silent integrity of the pictorial. Writing about Camille Corot, Paul Valéry warned, "We should apologize that we dare to speak about painting."

Yet, as Valéry also acknowledged, "There are important reasons for not keeping silent [since] all the arts live by words. Each work of art demands its response." Works of art initiate and provoke other works of art; the process is a source of art itself. Responses to a given work become part of the complex history of that work. There is also an intricate history of reciprocity and sibling rivalry between the arts, especially "the sister arts," poetry and painting. The writers in this collection are participating in a long occidental tradition of *ekphrasis,* the verbal description of pictorial or sculptural works of art. That tradition comes down to us in a more or less unbroken line from Homer and Theocritus to Keats and Shelley, Baudelaire and Gautier; it extends from Horace (whose famous phrase "Ut Pictura Poesis"—"as in painting, so in poetry"—has had a controversial history of its own) to William Carlos Williams and Marianne Moore, W. H. Auden and Randall Jarrell. Ekphrastic modes inevitably address—and sometimes challenge—the great divide between spatial and temporal experience, eye and ear, visual and verbal mediums. They brave the mystery dividing the seen from the unseen, image from text. They teach us to look and look again more closely. They dramatize with great intensity the actual experience of encounter. That is why the proper response to a work of visual art may well be an ode or an elegy, a meditative lyric, a lyrical meditation.

• • •

The range and diversity of this book are among its pleasures. The formal cornucopia includes short stories (Charles Baxter, Charles Johnson), aphoristic meditations (Susan Mitchell, Susan Stewart), and prose poems—or are they a kind of essay (Charles Simic, John Yau)? There is a splendid villanelle that mirrors elements in a Giorgio de Chirico painting (Mark Strand), a dramatic monologue in sonnet form (Ellen Bryant Voigt), a rich adaptation of a Japanese form, the *tanga* (Cynthia Macdonald). Richard Wilbur's consideration of transcendence in the work of Edgar Degas commences with a deft translation of a sonnet by the artist. The strategies diversify as Richard Howard apostrophizes Henri Fantin-Latour and Joyce Carol Oates projects the hidden thoughts—the interior reality—of the figures in *Nighthawks*. In "Listening" John Edgar Wideman ascribes to a painting by William Sydney Mount "something like the all-encompassing memory of music" wherein he hears—we hear—the agonizing tune of "Jim Crow" in the background. Like "The Man with the Blue Guitar," this piece suggests that a painting not only can be seen, but also entered and heard. Its context may speak volumes.

Time and again, these writings ask us to rearrange and redefine what we are viewing. They collect and focus our attention. "Let us look at this painting to which we are blinded by familiarity and parody," Guy Davenport says about Grant Wood's *American Gothic*. At times they surprise the painter in the self-conscious act of creating: "He paints what he sees, seeing what he paints," John Hollander reflects about Charles Sheeler's *The Artist Looks at Nature*. Rita Dove imagines Ivan Albright arranging his model and "applying paint/like a bandage to the open wound." The colors themselves are given

declarative voice in Adam Zagajewski's ecstatic lyric on Degas's *Millinery Shop*. Still others lead us to contemplate our own aesthetic principles and values. In thinking about Jules Breton's *Song of the Lark,* once voted the most popular painting in America, Amy Clampitt examines the reassuring innocence—ultimately the very function—of banality in art. John Updike's encounter with Claes Oldenburg's giant *Clothespin* becomes a graceful defense of the democratic spirit in Pop art.

There is something large and fundamental at stake in most of these pieces. They attend closely to artistic considerations—to the imperative of looking itself—but they are not aestheticized. "This is not an exhibition," the artist storms at the conclusion of Stanley Kunitz's metaphysical lyric "The Sea, That Has No Ending," "it's a life!" I think of Susan Sontag's passionate response—a lament really—to Francisco Goya's shockingly contemporary series *The Disasters of War*. "The problem is how not to avert one's glance," she writes in "Looking at the Unbearable," "How not to give way to the impulse to stop looking." This insistence on staring down—on reading—the unbearable is also at the heart of C. K. Williams's fierce response to the eternally cruel situation declared by Leon Golub's *Interrogation II*. Compellingly Gerald Stern finds Chaim Soutine's haunted self-portrait as a Jew dispersed through his painting of a dead fowl, and Francine Prose engages the problem of seeing her own image in Diane Arbus's photograph of two women in an Automat. In a highly personal poem, Li-Young Lee responds to a painting by his brother Li-Lin Lee.

The pieces in *Transforming Vision* are filled with intimacies attained, with reflections, refractions, revelations. The writings and the reproductions of works of art are before us here in their complex interplay and correspondence; this is a book of sights crossed by sounds, of visionary transformations.

Lobby of the Michigan Avenue
entrance to The Art Institute of
Chicago, 1903/05.

Galleries of European Painting
and Sculpture, c. 1987.

EXCERPT FROM "ON VARIOUS MINOR PAINTERS"

It is not unlikely that the Chicago Art Institute, with its splendid collection of casts and pictures, has done more for the people of the Middle West than any of the city's great industries. Every farmer boy who goes into the city on a freight train with his father's cattle and every young merchant who goes into the city to order his stock, takes a look at the pictures. There are thousands of people all over the prairies who have seen their first and only good pictures there. They select their favorites and go back to see them year after year. The men grow old and careworn themselves, but they find that these things of beauty are immortally joy-giving and immortally young. You will find hundreds of merchants and farmer boys all over Nebraska and Kansas and Iowa who remember Jules Breton's beautiful "Song of the Lark," and perhaps the ugly little peasant girl standing barefooted among the wheat fields in the early morning has taught some of these people to hear the lark sing for themselves.

Some of the most appreciative art criticisms I ever heard were made by two sunbrowned Kansas boys as they looked at George Inness' *Prairie Fire,* there in the Cyrus H. McCormick loan exhibition. Of all the lighthouses along the Great Harbor, there is none that throws its light so far.

Paderewski's theory of buying pictures and getting people to look at them has been exemplified in at least three cities in the United States: New York, Chicago and Pittsburgh. As a result those three cities contain nearly all the important private collections in the United States.

There is no reason why Pittsburgh, for instance, should display any greater interest in art than Kansas City or Denver or Omaha or San Francisco. It is not a city of culture; the city is entirely given over to manufacturing industries, and the only standard of success recognized is the pecuniary standard. But one thing Carnegie did; he bought pictures and got people to look at them.

Whether art itself can be propagated by infusion or no, has not been proven; but in some measure taste can be.

There is no reason why the common people of Chicago, the people who read Marie Corelli and go to see *The Pride of Jennico,* should know any more about pictures than the people of any other big city, but they do. Any stranger in the city who spends much time about the Art Institute must notice the comparatively enlightened conversation of the people who frequent the building on free days.

For some reason the institution is much nearer to the people of Chicago than the Metropolitan art gallery is to the people of New York. Perhaps it is because the spirit of caste is less perceptible in western cities, and the relations between employers and employees are more cordial. When any one of the Deerings or McCormicks buys an Inness or a Corot, he exhibits the picture in the Art Institute and their workmen drop in to have a look at it some Sunday and decide that they could have done something better with the money, if it had been theirs. The convenient and attractive location of the building may also have something to do with its popularity.

The collection of pictures is such that it would be impossible to cultivate a false or florid taste there.

(1895)

KILLING TIME

Between job interviews, I'd wander around the Art Institute, killing time. The Art Institute was on the park side of Michigan Avenue, across the street from the towering office buildings in which the employment agencies were situated. It felt soothing to drift among the paintings. Several had begun to feel like old friends. Visiting them beat sitting over a lukewarm coffee in some greasy spoon, spending another afternoon studying not only the Want Ads, but the faces of the others at the counter who sat nursing their coffees as they grimly studied the Want Ads too. By now, I spotted their faces everywhere. I'd become aware of an invisible army armed with Want Ads, pounding the pavement, knocking on doors, hoping opportunity would answer. It was an army without the consolation of camaraderie. I'd learned to recognize its unconscious salutes, its uniforms and ranks and outposts—personnel offices, coffee shops, and stands of public phones—from which its lonely campaigns were launched. I'd been looking for a job for over a month and was beginning to feel desperate.

The Art Institute was my base of operations. Its public phones were usually empty, and its restroom was modern and clean with a full-length mirror perfect for last minute inspections before heading out on an interview.

My first couple of weeks of job hunting, I'd hung out at the Public Library. Unlike the Art Institute, admission to the library was free. But the longer I'd gone without work, the more an old dread crept back into me: a feeling from high school, a memory of dreary Saturdays when, loaded with note cards for research papers that I was hopelessly behind on, I'd enter the Public Library only to end up wandering around lost, wasting the day. I remembered how, the summer before I'd started high school, my father had insisted that I spend a week at the library researching professions and the biographies of successful tycoons so that I'd have some sense of direction during my high school years and not live up to his nickname for me: The Dreamer. And I recalled how rather than doing what he'd asked, I'd only pretended to go to the library and instead had spent the money he'd given me at movies and record shops. Now, his dire predictions seemed to be coming true. My money was running out; I couldn't find a job. After a week of hanging around the library, I began to recognize the same set of regulars—people who carried their possessions in bags, or wore them all at once, who seemed to be living in the library stacks. Soon, I expected them to begin winking at me, giving me secret greetings I didn't want to recognize.

The public phones in the Public Library were always busy. In the old restrooms fluids pooled on the cracked terrazzo, and the homeless hung around inside, smoking, sometimes washing out their clothes in the plugged sinks. Even on the brightest days I began to notice the gray, gloomy cast of the marble corridors and flights of stairs. The reading rooms, dominated by the glow of green-shaded desk lamps, seemed worn as old railroad stations. There was a smell of musty pulp, of thumbed cloth covers, of too much print. At the long reading tables I could spot the displaced and dispossessed drowsing over enormous tomes or reading aloud to themselves as if engaged in debates with the complete works of Marx and Engels, Spengler, Tolstoy, Schopenhauer, while outside the windows cooing pigeons paced back and forth along the crusted slate ledges.

The Art Institute, by contrast, seemed flooded with light—not merely the light streaming from skylights or the track lights focused on paintings. The paintings themselves appeared to throw an internal light the way that oaks and maples seem aflame in fall, from the inside out. My favorite painters were the Impressionists. On days when it seemed as if I'd never find a job, when I was feeling desperate, I'd stand before their paintings and stare at them until it seemed I could almost step into their world, that if I closed my eyes and then opened them I'd find myself waking under the red coverlet in Van Gogh's *Bedroom at Arles*. I would open my eyes in a room of pastel light to find that one of Degas' dancers, who had been sleeping beside me, had discarded her chemise and was stepping into her morning bath. Or I would awaken already strolling without a care in and out of patches of precise shade, one of the Sunday crowd along the river on the island of *La Grande Jatte*. I wanted to be somewhere else, to be a dark blur waiting to board the Normandy train in the smoke-smudged *Saint-Lazare* station; I wanted a ticket out of my life, to be riding a train whose windows slid past with a landscape of haystacks in winter fields. It might be taking me to the beach of *Sainte-Adresse* where the fishing boats have been drawn up onto the sand and a man with a telescope and his daughter by his side looks out to sea, or to *Pourville* where the wind gusts along the cliff walk and a woman opens an orange parasol while white sails hardly taller than the white-capped waves pitch on the blue-green sea.

Yet, I would always end my walk through the paintings, standing before the diner in Edward Hopper's *Nighthawks*. Perhaps I needed its darkness to balance the radiance of the other paintings. It was night in Hopper's painting; the diner illuminated the dark city corner with a stark light it didn't seem capable of throwing on its own. Three customers sat at the counter as if waiting, not for something to begin, but rather to end, and I knew how effortless it would be to open my eyes and find myself waiting there, too.

(1990)

SAUL BELLOW
On Claude Monet, *Sandvika, Norway,* 1895

EXCERPT FROM *HUMBOLDT'S GIFT*

He was waiting between the lions in front of the Institute, exactly as expected in the cloak and blue velvet suit and boots with canvas sides. The only change was in his hair which he was now wearing in the Directoire style, the points coming down over his forehead. Because of the cold his face was deep red. He had a long mulberry-colored mouth, and impressive stature, and warts, and the distorted nose and leopard eyes. Our meetings were always happy and we hugged each other. "Old boy, how are you? One of your good Chicago days. I've missed the cold air in California. Terrific! Isn't it. Well, we may as well start right with a few of those marvelous Monets." We left attaché case, umbrella, sturgeon, rolls, and marmalade in the checkroom. I paid two dollars for admission and we mounted to the Impressionist collection. There was one Norwegian winter landscape by Monet that we always went to see straightaway: a house, a bridge, and the snow falling. Through the covering snow came the pink of the house, and the frost was delicious. The whole weight of snow, of winter, was lifted effortlessly by the astonishing strength of the light. Looking at this pure rosy snowy dusky light, Thaxter clamped his pince-nez on the powerful twisted bridge of his nose with a gleam of glass and silver and his color deepened. He knew what he was doing. With this painting his visit began on the right tone.

(1975)

16

ROBERT HAYDEN
On Claude Monet, *Water Lilies,* 1906

MONET'S "WATERLILIES"

(for Bill and Sonja)

Today as the news from Selma and Saigon
poisons the air like fallout,
    I come again to see
the serene great picture that I love.

Here space and time exist in light
the eye like the eye of faith believes.
    The seen, the known
dissolve in iridescence, become
illusive flesh of light
    that was not, was, forever is.

O light beheld as through refracting tears.
Here is the aura of that world
    each of us has lost.
Here is the shadow of its joy.

                              (1985)

DELMORE SCHWARTZ
On Georges Seurat, *A Sunday on La Grande Jatte—1884*, 1884–86

SEURAT'S SUNDAY AFTERNOON ALONG THE SEINE

To Meyer and Lillian Schapiro

What are they looking at? Is it the river?
The sunlight on the river, the summer, leisure,
Or the luxury and nothingness of consciousness?
A little girl skips, a ring-tailed monkey hops
Like a kangaroo, held by a lady's lead
(Does the husband tax the Congo for the monkey's keep?)
The hopping monkey cannot follow the poodle dashing ahead.

Everyone holds his heart within his hands:

A prayer, a pledge of grace or gratitude
A devout offering to the god of summer, Sunday and plenitude.

The Sunday people are looking at hope itself.

They are looking at hope itself, under the sun, free from the
    teething anxiety, the gnawing nervousness
Which wastes so many days and years of consciousness.

The one who beholds them, beholding the gold and green
Of summer's Sunday is himself unseen. This is because he is
Dedicated radiance, supreme concentration, fanatically
    threading
The beads, needles and eyes—at once!—of vividness and
    permanence.
He is a saint of Sunday in the open air, a fanatic disciplined
By passion, courage, passion, skill, compassion, love: the love
    of life and the love of light as one, under the sun, with the
    love of life.

Everywhere radiance glows like a garden in stillness
    blossoming.

Many are looking, many are holding something or someone
Little or big: some hold several kinds of parasols:
Each one who holds an umbrella holds it differently
One hunches under his red umbrella as if he hid
And looked forth at the river secretly, or sought to be
Free of all of the others' judgement and proximity.
Next to him sits a lady who has turned to stone, or become
    a boulder,
Although her bell-and-sash hat is red.
A little girl holds to her mother's arm
As if it were a permanent genuine certainty:
Her broad-brimmed hat is blue and white, blue like the river,
    like the sailboats white,
And her face and her look have all the bland innocence,
Open and far from fear as cherubims playing harpsichords.
An adolescent girl holds a bouquet of flowers
As if she gazed and sought her unknown, hoped-for, dreaded
    destiny.
No hold is as strong as the strength with which the trees,
Grip the ground, curve up to the light, abide in the warm
    kind air:
Rooted and rising with a perfected tenacity
Beyond the distracted erratic case of mankind there.
Every umbrella curves and becomes a tree,
And the trees curving, arise to become and be
Like the umbrella, the bells of Sunday, summer, and Sunday's
    luxury.

20

Assured as the trees is the strolling dignity
Of the bourgeois wife who holds her husband's arm
With the easy confidence and pride of one who is
—She is sure—a sovereign Victorian empress and queen.
Her husband's dignity is as solid as his *embonpoint*:
He holds a good cigar, and a dainty cane, quite carelessly.
He is held by his wife, they are each other's property,
Dressed quietly and impeccably, they are suave and grave
As if they were unaware or free of time, and the grave,
Master and mistress of Sunday's promenade—of everything!

—As they are absolute monarchs of the ring-tailed monkey.
If you look long enough at anything
It will become extremely interesting;
If you look very long at anything
It will become rich, manifold, fascinating:

If you can look at any thing for long enough,
You will rejoice in the miracle of love,
You will possess and be blessed by the marvellous blinding
   radiance of love, you will be radiance.

Selfhood will possess and be possessed, as in the
	consecration of marriage, the mastery of vocation, the
	mystery of gift's mastery, the deathless relation of parent-
	hood and progeny.
All things are fixed in one direction:
	We move with the Sunday people from right to left.

The sun shines
In soft glory
Mankind finds
The famous story
Of peace and rest, released for a little while from the tides of
	weekday tiredness, the grinding anxiousness
Of daily weeklong lifelong fear and insecurity,
The profound nervousness which in the depths of
	consciousness
Gnaws at the roots of the teeth of being so continually,
	whether in sleep or wakefulness,
We are hardly aware that it is there or that we might ever be
	free
Of its ache and torment, free and open to all experience.

The Sunday summer sun shines equally and voluptuously
Upon the rich and the free, the comfortable, the *rentier,* the
	poor, and those who are paralyzed by poverty.
Seurat is at once painter, poet, architect, and alchemist:
The alchemist points his magical wand to describe and hold
	the Sunday's gold,
Mixing his small alloys for long and long
Because he wants to hold the warm leisure and pleasure of the
	holiday
Within the fiery blaze and passionate patience of his gaze and
	mind
Now and forever: O happy, happy throng,
It is forever Sunday, summer, free: you are forever warm
Within his little seeds, his small black grains,
He builds and holds the power and the luxury
With which the summer Sunday serenely reigns.

—Is it possible? It is possible!—
Although it requires the labors of Hercules, Sisyphus, Flaubert,
	Roebling:
The brilliance and spontaneity of Mozart, the patience of a
	pyramid,
And requires all these of the painter who at twenty-five
Hardly suspects that in six years he will no longer be alive!
—His marvellous little marbles, beads, or molecules
Begin as points which the alchemy's magic transforms
Into diamonds of blossoming radiance, possessing and blessing
	the visual:
For look how the sun shines anew and newly, transfixed
By his passionate obsession with serenity
As he transforms the sunlight into the substance of pewter,
	glittering, poised and grave, vivid as butter,
In glowing solidity, changeless, a gift, lifted to immortality.

The sunlight, the soaring trees and the Seine
Are as a great net in which Seurat seeks to seize and hold
All living being in a parade and promenade of mild, calm
	happiness:
The river, quivering, silver blue under the light's variety,
Is almost motionless. Most of the Sunday people
Are like flowers, walking, moving toward the river, the sun,
	and the river of the sun.
Each one holds some thing or some one, some instrument
Holds, grasps, grips, clutches or somehow touches
Some form of being as if the hand and fist of holding and
	possessing,
Alone and privately and intimately, were the only genuine
	lock or bond of blessing.

A young man blows his flute, curved by pleasure's musical
	activity,
His back turned upon the Seine, the sunlight, and the
	sunflower day.
A dapper dandy in a top hat gazes idly at the Seine:
The casual delicacy with which he holds his cane
Resembles his tailored elegance.

He sits with well-bred posture, sleek and pressed,
Fixed in his niche: he is his own mustache.
A working man slouches parallel to him, quite comfortable,
Lounging or lolling, leaning on his elbow, smoking a
    meerschaum,
Gazing in solitude, at ease and oblivious or contemptuous
Although he is very near the elegant young gentleman.
Behind him a black hound snuffles the green, blue ground.
Between them, a wife looks down upon
The knitting in her lap, as in profound
Scrutiny of a difficult book. For her constricted look
Is not in her almost hidden face, but in her holding hands
Which hold the knitted thing as no one holds
Umbrella, kite, sail, flute or parasol.

This is the nervous reality of time and time's fire which turns
Whatever is into another thing, continually altering and
    changing all identity, as time's great fire burns (aspiring,
    flying and dying),
So that all things arise and fall, living, leaping and fading,
    falling, like flames aspiring, flowering, flying and dying—
Within the uncontrollable blaze of time and of history:
Hence Seurat seeks within the cave of his gaze and mind to
    find
A permanent monument to Sunday's simple delight; seeks
    deathless joy through the eye's immortality;
Strives patiently and passionately to surpass the fickle
    erratic quality of living reality.

Within this Sunday afternoon upon the Seine
Many pictures exist inside the Sunday scene:
Each of them is a world itself, a world in itself (and as a living
    child links generations, reconciles the estranged and aged
    so that a grandchild is a second birth, and the rebirth of
    the irrational, of those who are forlorn, resigned or
    implacable),
Each little picture links the large and small, grouping the big
Objects, connecting them with each little dot, seed or black
    grain

Which are as patterns, a marvellous network and tapestry,
Yet have, as well, the random freshness and radiance
Of the rippling river's sparkle, the frost's astonishing systems,
As they appear to morning's waking, a pure, white delicate
    stillness and minuet,
In December, in the morning, white pennants streaked upon
    the windowpane.

He is fanatical: he is at once poet and architect,
Seeking complete evocation in forms as strong as the Eiffel
    Tower,
Subtle and delicate too as one who played a Mozart sonata,
    alone, under the spires of Notre-Dame.
Quick and utterly sensitive, purely real and practical,
Making a mosaic of the little dots into a mural of the
    splendor of order:
Each micro pattern is the dreamed of or imagined
    macrocosmos
In which all things, big and small, in willingness and love
    surrender
To the peace and elation of Sunday light and sunlight's
    pleasure, to the profound measure and order of proportion
    and relation.

He reaches beyond the glistening spontaneity
Of the dazzled Impressionists who follow
The changing light as it ranges, changing, moment by
    moment, arranging and charming and freely bestowing
All freshness and all renewal continually on all that shows
    and flows.

Although he is very careful, he is entirely candid.
Although he is wholly impersonal, he has youth's frankness
    and, such is his candor,
His gaze is unique and thus it is intensely personal:
It is never facile, glib, or mechanical,
His vision is simple: yet it is also ample, complex, vexed, and
    profound
In emulation of the fullness of Nature maturing and enduring
    and toiling with the chaos of actuality.

An infinite variety within a simple frame:
Countless variations upon a single theme!
Vibrant with what soft soft luster, what calm joy!
This is the celebration of contemplation,
This is the conversion of experience to pure attention,
Here is the holiness of all the little things
Offered to us, discovered for us, transformed into the vividest
    consciousness,
After the shallowness or blindness of experience,
After the blurring, dirtying sooted surfaces which, since Eden
    and since birth,
Make all the little things trivial or unseen,
Or tickets quickly torn and thrown away
En route by rail to an ever-receding holiday:
—Here we have stopped, here we have given our hearts
To the real city, the vivid city, the city in which we dwell
And which we ignore or disregard most of the luminous day!

. . . Time passes: nothing changes, everything stays the same.
    Nothing is new
Under the sun. It is also true
That time passes and everything changes, year by year, day
    by day,
Hour by hour. Seurat's *Sunday Afternoon along the Seine* has
    gone away,
Has gone to Chicago: near Lake Michigan,
All of his flowers shine in monumental stillness fulfilled.
And yet it abides elsewhere and everywhere where images
Delight the eye and heart, and become the desirable, the
    admirable, the willed
Icons of purified consciousness. Far and near, close and far
    away
Can we not hear, if we but listen to what Flaubert tried to say,
Beholding a husband, wife and child on just such a day:
Ils sont dans le vrai! They are with the truth, they have found
    the way
The kingdom of heaven on earth on Sunday summer day.
Is it not clear and clearer? Can we not also hear
The voice of Kafka, forever sad, in despair's sickness trying
    to say:

"Flaubert was right: *Ils sont dans le vrai!*
Without forbears, without marriage, without heirs,
Yet with a wild longing for forbears, marriage, and heirs:
They all stretch out their hands to me: but they are too far
    away!"

                (1959)

WILLIAM MAXWELL
On Eugène Boudin, *Approaching Storm,* 1864

THE LITTLE BOUDIN BEACH SCENE

My wife comes from Portland, Oregon, and for a number of years after we were married we went to the West Coast by train. Between our arrival in Chicago on the New York Central and our departure on the Union Pacific there was just time for a visit to the Art Institute. The first time I saw the little Boudin beach scene, in a gallery devoted to nineteenth-century French painters, I cried out with pleasure. It also awakened the sleeping criminal in me, for it is only twenty-two by fourteen inches, roughly, and I saw myself putting it under my coat and walking down the marble staircase and out onto Michigan Avenue and hailing a cab. It is just as well that museum pictures are wired, because from time to time somebody is bound to think *If I don't have that painting where I can look at it every day, I will die . . .*

It is called *Approaching Storm,* and it was exhibited in the Salon of 1864. Napoleon III occupied the throne of France, though not very securely. It could have been a metaphor for the political situation between France and Germany, if Eugène Boudin had been that kind of painter.

The cloud bank has not yet blotted out the sunshine, which falls on two bathing machines in the center of the picture and a woman in a vast white crinoline. Her white jacket has a black trim. She has a furled white umbrella and is wearing a small black hat with a white veil, which the sea breeze is blowing from her face. Her dark hair is gathered in a large bun at the back of her neck—a fashion set by the Empress Eugénie. She is holding by the hand a little girl whose outfit is a copy in miniature of hers.

A long line of bathing machines frames the composition on the left. They are in deep shadow and are a dove gray. And essential. Without them it would look more or less like other Boudin beach scenes, of which there are a good many. The woman, the little girl, and a small terrier that clearly belongs to them are a cold zinc white. The two bathing machines in the center of the picture are a warmer white that is verging on ivory. Their wheels are resting on yellow sand.

My French dictionary doesn't give the word for "bathing machine," but I can't help thinking that either Lewis Carroll or Edward Lear had a hand in the naming of them. You undressed in the little house on wheels and a horse was put between the shafts and you were driven out beyond the shallow water to where it was deep enough to swim. And dived from the open door. And didn't have to wear a bathing suit. If it was Madame who was bathing and not Monsieur, the attendant gazed discreetly at the horizon.

I once knew a young Harvard professor who was so ardent an Anglophile that he imported a punt from England and poled his way up and down a small creek near Pomfret, Connecticut, but to the best of my knowledge bathing machines were never employed on any American beach. It must have been because they would have served no practical purpose. European beaches are, of course, rocky and rocks are painful to walk any great distance on.

What I love about this little Boudin is the mise-en-scène. The grouping of the figures could hardly be more theatrical. They are arranged in clusters, their heads close together, talking furiously. And there are many more women than men. The men are wearing black suits and, mostly, straw hats with a small curled brim—except for the man who with a raised arm is pointing to an ominous cloud bank over the ocean; he is wearing a derby. And how much everybody has on! The voluminous black-and-white ensemble of a woman in the left foreground is going to inspire one of Manet's finest canvases.

Boudin's seascapes were done in the open air, which may account for the hasty brushstrokes and the general freedom of the painting. If he had been as tight a painter as Canaletto, for example, one would have been able to make out what the

26

woman in the black cape and pale blue skirt is doing for the little girl in the scarlet dress. Or is it mere fuss? It reminds me of how, when I was a small child, my mother would moisten a corner of her handkerchief with spit and remove a smudge from my face. The color red is placed carefully throughout the picture—behind the woman in white, in a pile of clothing under a bathing machine, in the dress of a woman in the right foreground, and in the cape of a talker seated some distance behind her near a flagpole. There are five such poles, very tall with triangular pennants waving from the top. Are they territorial, or do they convey information about the bathing conditions?

In the year 1948, sightseeing, we went from Mont-Saint-Michel to Saint-Malo. German bombers had obliterated the picturesque medieval harbor front. The new buildings put up by the French government were of no interest so we went on, by bus, to the famous beach at Dinard. The sky was lead-colored. The striped tents were pretty but there was a cold wind, and the bathers sat with their backs to the water and looked mean and unfriendly. Congo natives wear more to cover their nakedness than these French bathers did. In less than a hundred years all that clothing—crinolines, capes, camisoles, corsets, corset covers, petticoats, scarves, shawls, hoods, hats with ostrich feathers, silk cords with tassels, ribbons, veils—was simply blown away. And with them feminine charm as it was understood by the Second Empire.

In the little Boudin, there is a patch of blue showing through an opening in the clouds. The sea birds have gone inland. How far away is the hotel verandah that the people must take refuge in before they are drenched to the skin? I figure the storm will break in about fifteen minutes. How well they all know each other! How much they are finding to say. What beautiful French (if one could only hear it). The chairs they are sitting on are not of the folding kind but sturdy, square, oak, one would say. Heavy, certainly. The chatter will go on until a sudden wind springs up and the first raindrops are felt. Then in alarm they will rise, gather up their things, and run for shelter, leaving the beach chairs to their fate.

The painter, grateful for every second that he is allowed to go on painting, is of the opinion that when the lightning flashes begin and thunder rolls across the sky it is going to be one hell of a storm.

HENRI FANTIN-LATOUR *UN COIN DE TABLE* (1873)

All those men have gone. Over a year
since they left the table where you have arranged
    matters, assortment of properties
that set the "natural" stage of *natures mortes,*
    the apparatus of your practiced
art, or at the very least the articles
    of your everlasting apprenticeship:

the consuetudinal cup and glass,
the former drained to show your skill, the latter
    filled, for the same purpose, with wine from
a pitcher that has perdured here eighteen months
    (though turned, now, to face the other way);
a cruet which is well-rehearsed, a compote
    covertly upstaged by that silver bowl . . .

You have shifted the rhododendrons
from the right (where they supplanted old Mérat
    who would not share a purposed *Hommage*
à Baudelaire with beasts of such behavior
    as the poets who stare in separate
lethargies past each other on the left:
    Rimbaud, Verlaine, abominable pair!)

to the foreground, lavish corollas
standing in for laureates of shameful life
    and for enshrined (and shaggy) lions
blameless in their oblivion ever since—
    now we name them only from the list
drawn up by the orderly Mlle Dubourg,
    whom you would marry in a few more years.

It was to maintain the new ménage
that you sold, in England, eight-hundred portraits
    of flowers! while sending to the Salon
voluted *fantaisies* that have duly turned
    to more hectares of blackened leather
than all the Wagnerites in Paris could buy.
    You kept your shameful secret (so you thought)

of those remunerative roses,
hollyhocks, pansies, peonies, whatever
    she brought in from the garden each day,
and went on portraying *ces messieurs* in all
    their grave coats, their cretaceous collars,
their gold watchfobs and their contemptuous stares:
    "Around the Piano," "In a Batignolles

Studio"—and all the while you knew
what you dared to acknowledge only in oils:
    these perennials and the power
to paint air around them which was all you had,
    all you needed. At the retrospective
of '06, *tout-Paris* was fluttered to find
    such flowers never seen in France before.

No lions here, and no Rhinemaidens,
just an empty table, its white cloth still creased,
    these months, as if fresh from the mangle,
the patient props and, wholly unjustified
    by any important theme or scheme,
not even a pot to grow in, these branches
    of rhododendron . . . This life . . . This art . . .

RICHARD WILBUR
On Edgar Degas, *Portrait after a Costume Ball*
(Portrait of Mme Dietz-Monnin), 1877/79, and *Ballet at the Paris Opéra, 1877*

DEGAS AND TRANSCENDENCE

Here is an attempted translation, done many years ago, of one of those sonnets that Degas took to writing in the latter 1880s:

> I think that, sure of the beauty of her repose,
> Indolent nature had in the former time
> Too dully slept, had grace not often come
> With gay and panting voice to bid her rise,
>
> And beaten then for her a pleasing measure,
> And with the motion of her speaking hands
> And twining of her fiery feet, commanded
> That she cavort before her, full of pleasure.
>
> Then come, my darlings, wear that rabble face,
> And do not wish for beauty's needless glow!
> Leap brazenly, my priestesses of grace!
>
> From the dance you gain a rareness in our eyes,
> An air heroic and remote. You know
> That queens are made of distance and disguise.

The sestet addresses the ballet-girls who are one of the major subjects of Degas the painter, but the poem bears also upon all of his most interesting work, even such a canvas as *Portrait after a Costume Ball.* Degas' poem is not impressed by given or natural beauty; what concerns it is art's joyous and difficult striving, by way of graceful movement, toward a condition of "rareness" or transcendence. That condition, as another of the sonnets tells, is precarious and brief: "Mais d'un signe toujours cesse le beau mystère."

A perfectionist who hated to declare any picture finished, Degas was especially devoted to such subjects—the café singer, the thoroughbred horse, the dancer—as involve hard training undergone in hopes of flawless performance, and the whipping of indolent flesh toward a moment of spirit. Does he paint such moments of assimilation to Le Beau or La Grâce? Seldom, or seldom in isolation from the grubby, prosaic world out of which those moments have risen. At any rate, one finds the fundamental drama of Degas' art in the sort of painting where one ballerina gracefully practices a position, while another, all adolescent gawkiness, sprawls wearily on a chair nearby; or in a painting like *Ballet at the Paris Opéra,* where the rehearsing dancers, transformed upon the lighted stage, are eyed from the dim pit by "male admirers and members of the orchestra."

Degas' disinclination to apotheosize is found not only in his ballet paintings, but everywhere else: he tends to see his subjects not afloat in vignetting, or complacently central, but involved in role and time and circumstance—in the process of their lives. It is this commitment to circumstance and process, I think—not the influence of photography, or a leaning toward abstraction—which makes for his more surprising compositions, wherein horses may half-leave the canvas, or a great bouquet cramp and overshadow a woman. The concern with motion and the momentary does not, of course, result in any expressive blurring; quite the contrary. Degas' Ingres-like drawing precisely captures the queenly arabesque of one dancer, the manner in which another tugs at her slipper, the contortion of a woman drying the back of her neck with a towel, the way in which one laundress bears down on the iron while another yawns in the heat and stretches; and in *Portrait after a Costume Ball* we indisputably have the expression, posture, and movement of a tired-but-happy hostess waving farewell to her guests. It is in his exact seizing of the split-second gesture (social, professional, habitual, artistic, or involuntarily expressive) that Degas is most universally human, and most transcends time.

JON STALLWORTHY
On Henri de Toulouse-Lautrec, *At the Moulin Rouge,* 1892/95

TOULOUSE-LAUTREC AT THE MOULIN ROUGE

'Cognac—more cognac for Monsieur Lautrec—
More cognac for the little gentleman,
Monster or clown of the Moulin—quick—
Another glass!'
                        The Can Can
Chorus with their jet net stockings
And their red heads rocking
Have brought their patrons flocking to the floor.
Pince-nez, glancing down from legs advancing
To five fingers dancing
Over a menu-card, scorn and adore
Prostitutes and skinny flirts
Who crossing arms and tossing skirts
High-kick—a quick
Eye captures all before they fall—
Quick lines, thick lines
Trace the huge ache under rouge.

'Cognac—more cognac!' Only the slop
Of a charwoman pushing her bucket and mop,
And the rattle of chairs on a table top.
The glass can fall no further. Time to stop
The charcoal's passionate waltzing with the hand.
Time to take up the hat, drag out the sticks,
And very slowly, like a hurt crab, stand:
With one wry bow to the vanished band,
Launch out with short steps harder than high kicks
Along the unspeakable inches of the street.
His flesh was his misfortune: but the feet
Of those whose flesh was all their fortune beat
Softly as the grey rain falling
Through his brain recalling
Marie, Annette, Jean-Claude and Marguerite.
                                    (1963)

EDGAR DEGAS: *THE MILLINERY SHOP*

Hats are innocent, bathed in the soft light
which smoothes the contours of objects.
A girl is working.
But where are brooks? Groves?
Where is the sensual laughter of nymphs?
The world is hungry and one day
will invade this tranquil room.
For the moment it contents itself
with ambassadors who announce:
I'm the ochre. I'm the sienna.
I'm the color of terror, like ash.
In me ships sink.
I'm the blue, I'm cold, I can be pitiless.
And I'm the color of dying, I'm patient.
I'm the purple (you don't see much of me),
for me triumphs, processions.
I'm the green, I'm tender,
I live in wells and in the leaves of birch trees.
The girl whose fingers are agile
cannot hear the voices, for she's mortal.
She thinks of the coming Sunday
and the rendezvous she has
with the butcher's son
who has coarse lips
and big hands
stained with blood.

(Translated by the author)

PAPE MOE (MYSTERIOUS WATER)

1

To be obsessed: to dwell with, to sit down upon like a bird on a nest—to brood. To make all flights from this nest, all forays, to keep hunting there. To seize this nest like prey and tear into it. Or to work at the way water wears away stone. Until the body is combed into the water and one with the weeds growing there, until the body is the grain of the current and the grain of the rock the current flows over and around. Not to budge from this place one is continually flowing from.

2

Not to budge until he has worked the same image in oil, in wood, in ink and watercolors. Is it that Gauguin cannot get enough of this thin trickle of light a woman is putting her mouth to? Or is it that he cannot get the image right? Cannot make the water, the rocks—what? Not to budge until he has carved and painted the wood. Not to budge until the woven paper has soaked up the ink, until the rocks are blue and the water is white.

3

The story he tells in *Noa Noa* seems to be the source of the visual image that obsessed him. But really, it is only one more variation, this time done in words. So now he needs language too, now there has to be a narrative. But the story is worth repeating if only because it suggests what Gauguin was unable to paint. He had been traveling around the island of Tahiti, sleeping under trees, eating shrimp served on banana leaves. Now he wakes at dawn, catatonic with attention. He is one bare room he lives in a week at a time. This is the back of his mind. Uncultivated, crude, unswept—his idea of paradise,

but also with a river wild and tangled with vegetation and a woman. The woman he sees in the bend of the river, a glimpse of her drinking from a waterfall. She is letting the water run between her breasts. Then she knows she is looked at. And vanishes. Or becomes the water or that eel coiled in the stones at the bottom of a pool.

4

In the oil Gauguin painted in 1893, the woman's position is awkward, her left hand leans heavily on a rock while her right arm, bent at the elbow, presses upward against a rock-like wall. The viewer feels the difficulty of her position, how uncomfortable her body must be as she leans forward to drink, as if this water can be had only at great physical cost, as if the body's pain and discomfort make the water more mysterious and deepen the joy of drinking this mustardy gold jet streaked with red. The water is solid, the woman might grasp it like a vine. The pool is a sensuous surface of scums and lilacs awash in dawn red, sunrise yellow.

5

There is a crime that needs to be committed. So he takes a knife to the paper and scrapes, working until the weave is almost worn down. Now there is light from behind the paper, the paper so thin, something tears through—the absence of image. Now the water has no sap or taste, no temperature. Now the water has no wetness, it is totally desiccated. A constant stream of dried up. Scratched into the paper. Incised. Or the water is the paper. The water is what no pigment has touched.

6

In place of the world, in place of memory, this ethereal, this ineffable, this immaterial—this paradise created wholly out of paper and ink and watercolor. So it was never the image that obsessed him. It was the paper he wanted to put his mouth to and this spermatic eel, this squirted out of—coil of white, rope twisted and convulsed.

7

Though at one time he must have thought he wanted to get his hands on the water and polish it, give it the shine that wood takes. Rub it with his hands until its currents flowed into the lines of his palms. He wanted to feel the water flowing through wood which itself flows as tree, but more slowly. The quick pace of the river made sluggish in the tree growing up through his hands. He wanted to polish his hands on that water. In the wood relief, carved around 1893, the water tumbles down like the hair of a woman bending forward, shaking all the long thick lengths of out in front of her. This is the water a man drinks from, for surely the sturdy figure in the relief is a man.

8

So there never was a woman drinking from the river Punuru. There was this man with sturdy shoulders and broad feet. And the man—the man was glimpsed in a photo taken by Charles Spitz. There is nothing mysterious about the water in the photo, it flows from a metal pipe. And the pipe, the stream of water issuing from it, the man—they are as blatant and inter-esting as telephone poles.

9

In the watercolor all sense of narrative has been removed. Even place is in question. The woman is awash in, floats in what she is drinking. But what she drinks is no longer pigment: it is the paper's corporeality, as if Gauguin were thirsting less for the image of water and more for the medium itself. As if the image of water were only a pretext.

10

The interactions of watercolor and ink with paper. The saturation of the paper, the way the images are drawn into it, either about to disappear into the fertile region behind the paper or about to emerge. This movement, this emergence, this shining forth—or this fading. Like a woman who appears and disappears. Only now the woman is hardly necessary. It is enough to feel the water soaking in as a leaf would feel it, as soil would. To feel the paper drinking in. To put his mouth to the mouth of the paper as it drinks in.

11

Placelessness. Dislocation. Where else is paradise but in the amorphousness of becoming?

CYNTHIA MACDONALD
On Mary Cassatt, *Woman Bathing*, 1891

MARY CASSATT'S TWELVE HOURS IN THE PLEASURE QUARTER

1 *Woman Bathing*
What is in back of the back?
Pleasure hidden behind flesh. Screened from view,
screened as if by gold squares. Paper.
Even the mirror reflects only thin
hair, leaving excess to bloom underfoot.

2 *Utamaro's Yoshiwara District*
Silk covers the moon's face and
scenes unfold before it, a fan unfurls
displaying reds and purples,
*Two Courtesans And A Child; Two Beauties
And A Young Man Beside A Cherry Tree.*

3 *Shared Studios*
Degas took her on. She took
him on. Imagine! This never girlish
girl from Philadelphia.
Colors fuse, no two alike. Fingerprints.
Miss M. Cassatt announces she's at home.

4 *The Country House: Seine-et-Oise*
Prints streaming down, a river
of prints hung in the hall "that leads out to
the cold glass-paned verandah
where hung the Utamaros and one or
two Hokusais," a guest's memoir recounts.

5 *Retroussage: Creative Wiping*
Water trickles in the cleft
of breasts. A shudder of pleasure, "how warm
it is today." Mary wipes
the ink out of the lines, dragging ink, black
as Japanese hair. Red hair: Retroussage.

6 *Daily Life*
Why is she washing? To thin
The aquatint? To wash off brains laved in
melted butter, jugged hare,
the sour milk of baby's spit-up, ink,
or paint, or juice of mutton, or semen?

7 *The Great Fire*
Tangerine, burnt orange, rust
ocher, orange madder: eight of the set
of ten suffused with shades of
orange. Flame. The Pittsburgh of her birth, sky
fused to firestorms. Wet, fugitive blue.

8 *"Stop-out" Work and Burnishing*
Degas inquires, "This back, did
you draw this?" He stands in front of *Woman
Bathing.* A single stroke, a stroke
of genius, a brush with common life, a
round, around a slowly growing nipple.

43

9 *Gifts*

"Retrouver, retrouver," cries
Mary's parrot, Coco. Degas brings her
    irises (though he hates cut
flowers) and a sonnet worked upon for
weeks: *Perroquet, à Miss Cassatt.* She smiles.

10 *Printing*

Four states for this print woman,
bathing. Inked *à la poupée* in green and light brown,
    special wiping, blued copper.
the hair and leaves rebitten, darkening them.
Drypoint amidst seduction of the bath.

11 *Impressionists and Bathing*

In back of the back? Baths with
Renoir, Degas, and Seurat—the pleasure
    quarter. A woman's glass, face
effaced, rubbed impressions of a print, still
wet. Suffusing light the skin drinks in.

12 *The Art Institute*

Hung on a wall, private parts
turned away, a woman by a woman
    scoops water from the moon,
her fingers twined in floating irises.
Two beauties, and a man and baby watch.

AFTERWORDS

Cassatt owned a few prints by Hokusai and a substantial number by Utamaro, including some of the series of twelve set in the pleasure quarter of Yoshiwara. It is generally agreed that this sequence of scenes from everyday life—though his prints depicted courtesans and actors—was the strongest influence on Cassatt's sequence of ten depicting women engaged in their daily tasks and errands. The passion with which she responded to the Japanese ukiyo-e is revealed in her letter to Berthe Morisot: "You could come here to dine and then we could go to see the Japanese prints at the Beaux Arts. Seriously, *you must not* miss that. For you, who wishes to make color prints, you could not dream of anything more beautiful. I already dream of it and of nothing besides color on copper. Fantin was there the 1st day I went and he was ecstatic. And Tissot was also there."

• • •

Degas and Cassatt were passionately involved with one another for many years. But no one now knows if they were lovers or if the consummation was purely artistic. Before she died, Cassatt burned his letters to her. Most of those who knew them believed that they were friends but not lovers. There was, and still is, a lot of speculation of the "did they or didn't they" variety. In 1944 my mother, who usually got her gossip right, announced as we stood in front of a painting by Cassatt that Cassatt had remained a virgin all her life, "in spite of all those mother-holding-a-child paintings."

• • •

Mary Cassatt's Twelve Hours in the Pleasure Quarter is an adaptation of the Japanese form, the *tanga,* with the syllable count expanded slightly to allow for the differences between sentence formation in Japanese and English.

• • •

Renoir, Degas, Seurat, and Cassatt all depicted bathers. A number of these works are in The Art Institute of Chicago's collection.

PATRICIA HAMPL
On Henri Matisse, *Woman Before an Aquarium*, 1921

WOMAN BEFORE AN AQUARIUM

The goldfish ticks silently,
little finned gold watch
on its chain of water,
swaying over the rivulets of the brain,
over the hard rocks and spiny shells.

The world is round, distorted
the clerk said when I insisted
on a round fishbowl.
Now, like a Matisse woman,
I study my lesson slowly,
crushing a warm pinecone
in my hand, releasing
the resin, its memory of wild nights,
my Indian back crushing
the pine needles, the trapper
standing over me, his white-dead skin.

Fear of the crushing,
fear of the human smell.
A Matisse woman always wants
to be a mermaid,
her odalisque body
stretches pale and heavy
before her and the exotic wall hangings;
the only power of the woman:
to be untouchable.

But dressed, a simple Western face,
a schoolgirl's haircut, the plain desk
of ordinary work, she sits
crushing the pinecone of fear,
not knowing it is fear.
The paper before her is blank.

The aquarium sits like a lantern,
a green inner light, round
and green, a souvenir
from the underworld,
its gold residents opening and closing
their wordless mouths.

I am on the shore of the room,
glinting inside
with the flicker of water,
heart ticking with the message
of biology to a kindred species.
The mermaid—not the enchantress,
but the mermaid of double life—
sits on the rock, combing
the golden strands of human hair,
thinking as always
of swimming.

(1978)

EXCERPT FROM *JOAN MIRÓ: LIFE AND WORK*

Another nude, *Nude with Bird and Flower,* exists only as an item in the catalogue of the Dalmau exhibition. The last of these representations of women is the *Portrait of Juanita Obrador* of about 1917. The young lady's head and shoulders appear against a background of wallpaper whose pattern incorporates flowers and a lozenge-type motif. As in the case of Ricart's pajamas, the artist has made much of the black and white stripes of the blouse while the background is a uniformly intense, indefinable pink—a sort of degraded purple—which more or less contaminates every part of the picture. The face, again, seems to have been hewn with some primitive hatchet. The green pupils of the eyes and the brutal accentuation of every feature make it a terrible face. It expresses not so much sadness or despair as some eternity of suffering, endured as fate.

(1962)

TWO LADIES AT THE AUTOMAT (NEW YORK CITY)

I can shut my eyes and see perfectly the first Diane Arbus photo I ever saw: the mournful transvestite with the penciled eyebrows and the long skinny head full of curlers. I was a sheltered girl of sixteen. My life was nothing like that guy's. So why should I have felt that I was looking in a mirror?

Maybe it was the curlers. In that other life, teenage life, I had learned to sleep on wire brushes, so right there the cross-dresser and I had one weird perversion in common. But it was more than beauty martyrdom. It was the expression in his eyes, a look you weren't supposed to see, though you glimpsed it in mirrors sometimes when the mirror caught you by surprise. It thrilled me to see, in those brimming eyes, a feeling so inchoate and profound I wouldn't have known how to talk about it then; I wouldn't have, and still wouldn't.

Thirty years later I get the same eerie chill from *Two Ladies at the Automat (New York City)*. It is another chill of resemblance, though my loved ones would be quick to reassure me that— and really, anyone could probably see that obviously—I look nothing, nothing in the world like either of these two ladies.

How beautifully dressed and theatrical they are in their carefully coordinated and stylishly accessorized outfits. Nothing is left to chance here, not their manicures or coiffures nor the delicate heartbreaking angles at which they tip their cigarettes. Nothing is accidental except the head-on collision with age.

Anyone who knows me knows that my friends don't look like that, either. So why should I see these ladies and think: There I am, with my friends! Again it's a glimmer in the eyes, another scary mix. They are at once so jaunty and so terribly anxious.

I am younger than the two ladies are in the photo, certainly younger than they are now. (Most likely they have vanished, like the Automats, those shiny cuckoo clocks stuffed with pie that so delighted me as a child.) And my sense of fashion could hardly be more different: I wear black clothes, high heels or cowboy boots, and I like to think a good haircut. I bite my nails, don't smoke, my taste in jewelry runs to vintage rhinestone. But the second hand on my watch is a tiny spider that ticks around a web; my metallic pea-green Doc Martens come from a store where *tout* junior high shops. Are those touches my leopard-skin pillbox hat, my pinky ring, my black Cossack hat, the scarf tied with more encoded meanings than a Japanese obi? What we have in common, the ladies and I, is not the look, but the effort.

People who don't like Diane Arbus's work call her a voyeur, a cold-hearted, cold-eyed exploiter of harmless perverts and geeks. But why have I never seen her photos as pictures of freaks, exactly? Her best photos seem to me to be mutant crosses between self-portraiture and fashion photography, two genres which, like much art, contain elements of exploitation, but which are way down the exploitation scale from shots of innocent creeps tricked into goggling at the camera.

Unlike Avedon and other photographers who often judge subjects by their clothing, Arbus shows us clothing as self-expression, as art. The planning and labor-intensive hours that went into the costumes these women selected to grace the Automat that day, the hats, suits, watches, the jewelry— it makes us want to applaud, or weep. Her camera is not judgmental, detached, though it compels us to acknowledge that at some points we are creatures of fashion caught in the oncoming headlights.

Diane Arbus has given us images we remember, we can't shake. When I mentioned the cross-dresser in curlers . . . Reader, you knew what he looks like, just as you can see the solemn twins in their dark dresses and lace collars, and the boy with the American flag. She has given us images that, like certain classic stories, pieces of music, or paintings, recede or

come into focus at critical points in our lives. My older son was a huge baby; for months I joked nervously about Eddie Carmel, Diane Arbus's Jewish giant, inclining like a sunflower down toward his puzzled, elderly parents. Eventually my husband asked me to cut out the Eddie Carmel jokes. As I write this, my son is nearly six-feet tall and apparently still growing.

Once it was the transvestite, then the giant, and now it's *Two Ladies at the Automat (New York City)* that I can summon up inside my eyelids. I shut my eyes and study them, poised beside the stone table at which there is no coffee or food, unless we count the salt and pepper. Have they finished eating or will they now begin? I know where their jauntiness comes from, their courage and their anxiety. For now, at least, they seem remote, though we are rapidly getting closer. Each passing minute nibbles away at the distance between us.

CARL SANDBURG
On Auguste Rodin, *The Walking Man,* c. 1900

 THE WALKING MAN OF RODIN

Legs hold a torso away from the earth.
And a regular high poem of legs is here.
Powers of bone and cord raise a belly and lungs
Out of ooze and over the loam where eyes look and ears hear
And arms have a chance to hammer and shoot and run motors.
        You make us
        Proud of our legs, old man.

And you left off the head here,
The skull found always crumbling neighbor of the ankles.

(1916)

EXCERPT FROM *THE SONG OF THE LARK*

One bleak day in February, when the wind was blowing clouds of dirt like a Moonstone sandstorm, dirt that filled your eyes and ears and mouth, Thea fought her way across the unprotected space in front of the Art Institute and into the doors of the building. She did not come out again until the closing hour. In the street-car, on the long cold ride home, while she sat staring at the waistcoat buttons of a fat strap-hanger, she had a serious reckoning with herself. She seldom thought about her way of life, about what she ought or ought not to do; usually there was but one obvious and important thing to be done. But that afternoon she remonstrated with herself severely. She told herself that she was missing a great deal; that she ought to be more willing to take advice and to go to see things. She was sorry that she had let months pass without going to the Art Institute. After this she would go once a week.

The Institute proved, indeed, a place of retreat, as the sand hills or the Kohlers' garden used to be; a place where she could forget Mrs. Andersen's tiresome overtures of friendship, the stout contralto in the choir whom she so unreasonably hated, and even, for a little while, the torment of her work. That building was a place in which she could relax and play, and she could hardly ever play now.

• • •

It was with a lightening of the heart, a feeling of throwing off the old miseries and old sorrows of the world, that she ran up the wide staircase to the pictures. There she liked best the ones that told stories. . . . She loved, too, a picture of some boys bringing in a newborn calf on a litter, the cow walking beside it and licking it. The Corot which hung next to this painting she did not like or dislike; she never saw it.

But in that same room there was a picture—oh, that was the thing she ran upstairs so fast to see! That was her picture.

She imagined that nobody cared for it but herself, and that it waited for her. That was a picture indeed. She liked even the name of it, "The Song of the Lark." The flat country, the early morning light, the wet fields, the look in the girl's heavy face—well, they were all hers, anyhow, whatever was there. She told herself that that picture was "right." Just what she meant by this, it would take a clever person to explain. But to her the word covered the almost boundless satisfaction she felt when she looked at the picture.

(1915)

AMY CLAMPITT
On Jules Breton, *The Song of the Lark,* 1884

THE SONG OF THE LARK

Chicago, in my earliest memory, was the place to which my father traveled once a year with a load of hogs, and returned with a few presents that had, for me, the glamor of all store-bought merchandise. It would have been in an especially profitable year, before the onset of the hard times that were to dominate my growing up, that he brought back a framed reproduction of *The Song of the Lark.* I don't remember a time before the advent of its reassuring banality—for what indeed is banality, in its root sense of proclaiming what is done and not done, but reassurance?

In some way, to my own starved and wistful consciousness, that picture *was* Chicago. Hog Butcher for the World, Freight Handler to the Nation—yes, Chicago was that as well. After I'd somehow made the overland leap from Iowa to New York, the ultimate metropolis, Chicago became a place of changing trains, with a half-day wait during which I ritually made my way to the Art Institute. I'd known that the framed image of a silhouetted peasant girl on the wall of the dining room at home had come from there; but I never saw the original until a few years ago—and then only from a distance, stunned as I was, for all the extraneous reasons that are the despair of our aesthetic monitors, out of coming any nearer. Years before that moment, a reference had found its way into a poem I'd written:

> High art
> with a stiff neck—an upright Steinway
> bought in Chicago; a chromo of a Hobbema
> tree-avenue, of Millet's imagined peasant . . .

What I hadn't known, and what even then I did not learn, was that the painter wasn't Millet at all; it was Jules Breton.

How can such a mistake have originated? In the larger scheme of banality (as nearly as I can now reconstruct it)

Millet's was the bigger name. *The Man with the Hoe* was the work for which he was famous.

> Bowed by the weight of centuries he leans
> Upon his hoe and gazes on the ground,
> The emptiness of ages in his face,
> And on his back the burden of the world.

So Edwin Markham had written, with that painting in mind; and *he* is remembered for it chiefly in much the same way, on this side of the Atlantic, Jules Breton is remembered for his barefoot peasant—head up, a sickle in her hand, and behind her, cloven by the horizon, an immense red sun. I am disconcerted to be told in print that it is a *setting* sun. Can Shakespeare have been mistaken?—the banality of "Hark, Hark, the Lark," as set by Schubert and recorded by an operatic tenor whose name now escapes me (can it have been Richard Crooks?) having been fixed in my memory for about as long as the glassed-in scene on the dining-room wall. Of course there is also Romeo apprehending "It is the lark, the herald of the morn"—though it must be quickly added that Shelley imagined otherwise:

> The pale purple even
>   Melts around thy flight,
> Like a star of Heaven,
>   In the broad daylight
> Thou art unseen, but yet I hear thy shrill delight . . .

That I myself once, on a Greek island, heard skylarks after sunset is beside the point. Surely, having stooped all day to wield that sickle, the limberest peasant would not be standing erect, or have bothered to listen for anything so far above the ground. If a setting sun is truly what the painter intended, my impulse

is to say shame on him, because he must be lying—deliberately, and with the dubious intent of making up to somebody or other. Uplift of this specious sort is well known to have its own utility, with a dollar value in the offing.

Messages of uplift seem in retrospect to have been a kind of nineteenth-century specialty, and nowhere more than in these (more or less) United States. A tincture of countless weekly exhortations from the pulpit is unmistakable, for example, in the letters of Emily Dickinson. Her poetry is another matter; but it can be said in general that the drawing of homiletic conclusions seeped into very much of what verse or prose, got written, so indelibly that even now the lurking stain is expunged only with an effort—and not always successfully at that. Here is Richard Brettell, in the 1980s, on the painting in question:

> The lark itself is so small and so distant as it flies through the evening sky that, were it not for the title, most viewers would never be encouraged to find it. However, every search for the lark is ultimately successful, and when we find it, the silence of the painting is interrupted by the tiny fleck in the sky, whose gentle song, with its unmistakable message of hope, we can almost hear.

And one can almost hear the unction in the voice of any Protestant clergyman who might seize on all this as a neat elaboration of St. Paul in his Epistle to the Hebrews: "Now faith is the substance of things hoped for, the evidence of things not seen."

Such an observation, at the tag end of this bewildering century, comes all too easily at the expense of whatever sounds in the least didactic: too many assurances, too easily arrived at, have put not a few of us in a mood to doubt whether there is a lesson to be drawn from anything much. It was not always so. Wordsworth began his own address to a skylark with a fairly straightforward piece of observation—

> . . . while the wings aspire, are heart and eye
> Both with thy nest upon the dewy ground?
> Thy nest which thou canst drop into at will,
> Those quivering wings composed, that music still?—

but concluded on a homiletic note:

> Type of the wise who soar, but never roam;
> True to the kindred points of Heaven and Home:

The lines, it is true, date to the later, increasingly didactic phase in Wordsworth's career. But even the rebel Shelley did not shun the possibility of being taught. Where the skylark was concerned, he positively invited it:

> Better than all measures
>   Of delightful sound,
> Better than all treasures
>   That in books are found,
> Thy skill to poet were, thou scorner of the ground!
>
> Teach me half the gladness
>   That thy brain must know,
> Such harmonious madness
>   From my lips would flow
> The world should listen—as I am listening now.

What the poet invites is not what Wordsworth thought he'd found, namely instruction on how to live wisely. It is something more specific, even technical: how to be a better poet. Or no, that isn't quite accurate, it's how to reach a wider audience, which may or may not be the same thing. One may, a bit wickedly, go on to ask why Shelley in particular wanted the world to listen if not for the purpose of teaching it something—and find oneself arguing on the side of purely technical instruction. To do a thing as well as possible, regardless of extraneous considerations, may just possibly, after all, have been what Jules Breton was aiming at. His career—once again according to Richard Brettell—"got off to a dramatic start in the 1850s, when his immense peasant genre pictures received considerably more favorable notice than those of the older—and more gifted— Jean François Millet." By the time he painted *The Song of the Lark,* in 1884, we are told,

> Breton himself had become increasingly interested in effects of light and atmosphere as his career continued, and he could never have conceived of such a composition, with its figure lit from behind, in the earlier years of his career. Indeed, Breton, too, for all

his aesthetic conservatism, was moved to expand his own art by the example of the young Impressionists, whose art he despised.

How Mr. Brettell knows this he does not say. That one can learn at an unconscious level from what one consciously resists, as a general proposition, I have no doubt. Where art is concerned, much that goes on is subliminal. Of what it is in a particular painting that draws a viewer, the viewer may have only a dim and unstated notion. Was it those effects of light and atmosphere that caused James J. Hill of St. Paul, Minnesota, on a visit to the Paris Salon of 1885, to stop and consider *The Song of the Lark?* All we know is that, in Mr. Brettell's words, he "snapped [it] up." Within a decade it had passed into the collection of Henry Field and thence into the galleries of The Art Institute of Chicago, whence the image of it seeped, or filtered, by whatever Pointillist process such things may be said to occur, into what is referred to as the popular consciousness. How many prints in due course found their way into how many households, I can only guess. In the rural hamlet where I grew up, I must have seen it in half a dozen.

Is this a good or a bad thing?

It is all too easy to sneer at banality, and at the innocence that informs it. That innocence may in time learn to be wary of the derivative, the too-glibly (if not altogether wrongly) identified. It may learn in due course to look again and, unintimidated by whatever aesthetic monitors, to value for its own sake what they have taught it halfway to despise.

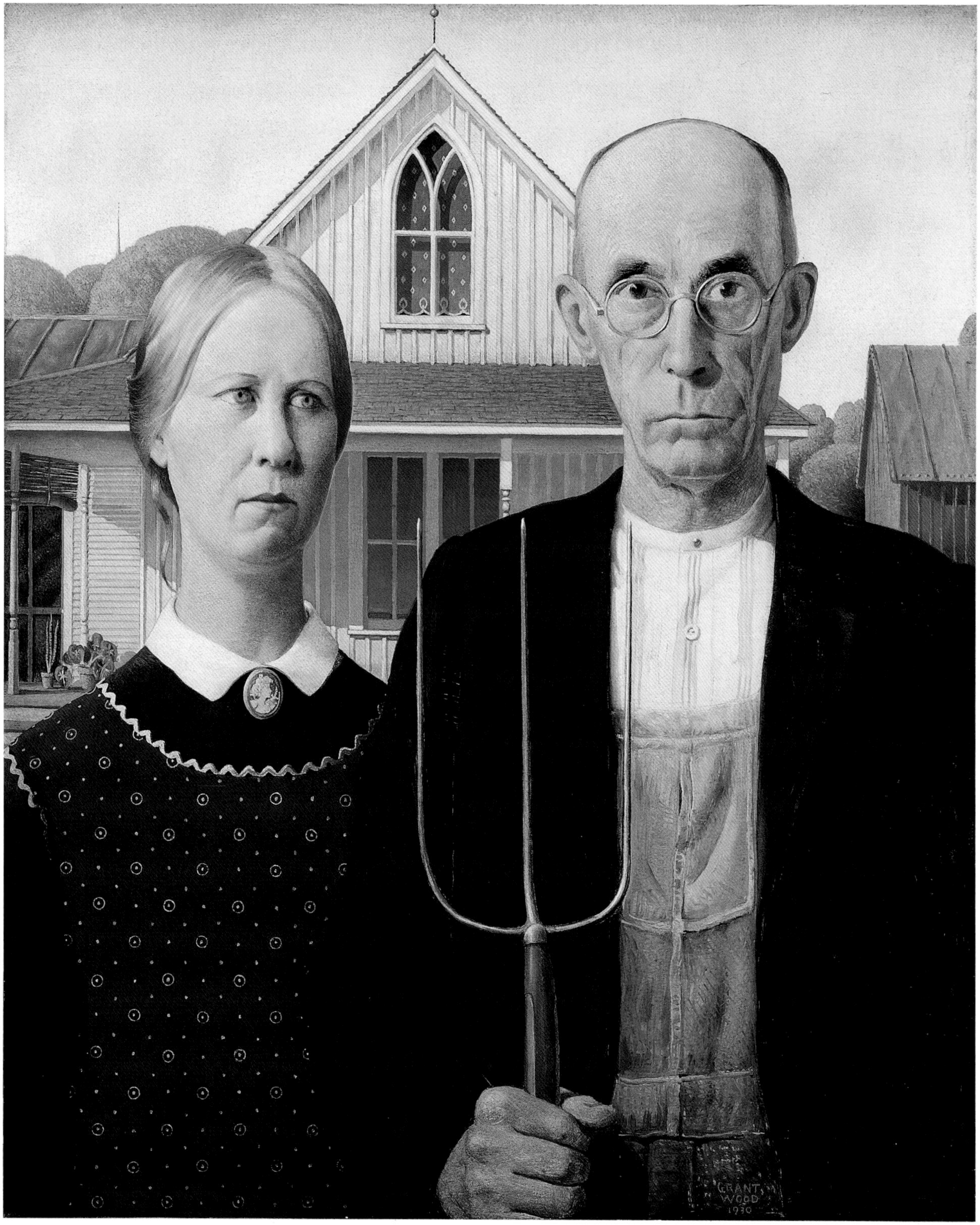
GRANT WOOD
1930

EXCERPT FROM *THE GEOGRAPHY OF THE IMAGINATION*

A geography of the imagination would extend the shores of the Mediterranean all the way to Iowa.

Eldon, Iowa—where in 1929 Grant Wood sketched a farmhouse as the background for a double portrait of his sister Nan and his dentist, Dr. B. H. McKeeby, who donned overalls for the occasion and held a rake. Forces that arose three millennia ago in the Mediterranean changed the rake to a pitchfork, as we shall see.

Let us look at this painting to which we are blinded by familiarity and parody. In the remotest distance against this perfect blue of a fine harvest sky, there is the Gothic spire of a country church, as if to seal the Protestant sobriety and industry of the subjects. Next there are trees, seven of them, as along the porch of Solomon's temple, symbols of prudence and wisdom.

Next, still reading from background to foreground, is the house that gives the primary meaning of the title, *American Gothic,* a style of architecture. It is an example of a revolution in domestic building that made possible the rapid rise of American cities after the Civil War and dotted the prairies with decent, neat farmhouses. It is what was first called in derision a balloon-frame house, so easy to build that a father and his son could put it up. It is an elegant geometry of light timber posts and rafters requiring no deep foundation, and is nailed together. Technically, it is, like the clothes of the farmer and his wife, a mail-order house, as the design comes out of a pattern-book, this one from those of Alexander Davis and Andrew Downing, the architects who modified details of the Gothic Revival for American farmhouses. The balloon-frame house was invented in Chicago in 1833 by George Washington Snow, who was orchestrating in his invention a century of mechanization that provided the nails, wirescreen, sash-windows, tin roof, lathe-turned posts for the porch, doorknobs, locks, and hinges—all standard pieces from factories.

We can see a bamboo sunscreen—out of China by way of Sears Roebuck—that rolls up like a sail: nautical technology applied to the prairie. We can see that distinctly American feature, the screen door. The sash-windows are European in origin, their glass panes from Venetian technology as perfected by the English, a luxury that was a marvel of the eighteenth century, and now as common as the farmer's spectacles, another revolution in technology that would have seemed a miracle to previous ages. Spectacles begin in the thirteenth century, the invention of either Salvino degl'Armati or Alessandro della Spina; the first portrait of a person wearing specs is of Cardinal Ugone di Provenza, in a fresco of 1352 by Tommaso Barisino di Modena. We might note, as we are trying to see the geographical focus that this painting gathers together, that the center for lens grinding from which eyeglasses diffused to the rest of civilization was the same part of Holland from which the style of the painting itself derives.

Another thirteenth-century invention prominent in our painting is the buttonhole. Buttons themselves are prehistoric, but they were shoulder-fasteners that engaged with loops. Modern clothing begins with the buttonhole. The farmer's wife secures her Dutch Calvinist collar with a cameo brooch, an heirloom passed down the generations, an eighteenth-century or Victorian copy of a design that goes back to the sixth century B.C.

She is a product of the ages, this modest Iowa farm wife: she has the hair-do of a mediaeval madonna, a Reformation collar, a Greek cameo, a nineteenth-century pinafore.

Martin Luther put her a step behind her husband; John Knox squared her shoulders; the stock-market crash of 1929 put that look in her eyes.

The train that brought her clothes—paper pattern, bolt cloth, needle, thread, scissors—also brought her husband's bib overalls, which were originally, in the 1870s, trainmen's workclothes designed in Europe, manufactured here for J. C. Penney, and disseminated across the United States as the railroads connected city with city. The cloth is denim, from Nîmes in France, introduced by Levi Strauss of blue-jean fame. The design can be traced to no less a person than Herbert Spencer, who thought he was creating a utilitarian one-piece suit for everybody to wear. His own example was of tweed, with buttons from crotch to neck, and his female relatives somehow survived the mortification of his sporting it one Sunday in St. James Park.

His jacket is the modification of that of a Scots shepherd which we all still wear.

Grant Wood's Iowans stand, as we might guess, in a pose dictated by the Brownie box camera, close together in front of their house, the farmer looking at the lens with solemn honesty, his wife with modestly averted eyes. But that will not account for the pitchfork held as assertively as a minuteman's rifle. The pose is rather that of the Egyptian prince Rahotep, holding the flail of Osiris, beside his wife Nufrit—strict with

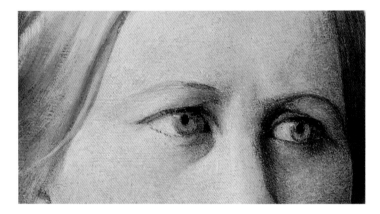

pious rectitude, poised in absolute dignity, mediators between heaven and earth, givers of grain, obedient to the gods.

This formal pose lasts out 3000 years of Egyptian history, passes to some of the classical cultures—Etruscan couples in terra cotta, for instance—but does not attract Greece and Rome. It recommences in northern Europe, where (to the dismay of the Romans) Gaulish wives rode beside their husbands in the war chariot. Kings and eventually the merchants of the North repeated the Egyptian double portrait of husband and wife: van Eyck's Meester and Frouw Arnolfini; Rubens and his wife

Helena. It was this Netherlandish tradition of painting middle-class folk with honor and precision that turned Grant Wood from Montparnasse, where he spent two years in the 1920s trying to be an American post-Impressionist, back to Iowa, to be our Hans Memling.

If Van Gogh could ask, "Where is my Japan?" and be told by Toulouse-Lautrec that it was Provence, Wood asked himself the whereabouts of his Holland, and found it in Iowa.

Just thirty years before Wood's painting, Edwin Markham's poem "The Man with the Hoe" had pictured the farmer as a peasant with a life scarcely different from that of an ox, and called on the working men of the world to unite, as they had nothing to lose but their chains. The painting that inspired Markham was one of a series of agricultural subjects by Jean François Millet, whose work also inspired Van Gogh. A digging fork appears in five of Van Gogh's pictures, three of them variations on themes by Millet, and all of them are studies of grinding labor and poverty.

And yet the Independent Farmer had edged out the idle aristocrat for the hand of the girl in Royal Tyler's "The Contrast," the first native American comedy for the stage, and in Emerson's "Concord Hymn" it is a battle-line of farmers who fire the shot heard around the world. George III, indeed, referred to his American colonies as "the farms," and the two Georges of the Revolution, Hanover and Washington, were proudly farmers by etymology and in reality.

The window curtains and apron in this painting are both calico printed in a reticular design, the curtains of rhombuses, the apron of circles and dots, the configuration Sir Thomas Browne traced through nature and art in his *Garden of Cyrus,* the quincunxial arrangement of trees in orchards, perhaps the first human imitation of a phyllotaxis, acknowledging the symmetry, justice, and divine organization of nature.

Curtains and aprons are as old as civilization itself, but their presence here in Iowa implies a cotton mill, a dye works, a roller press that prints calico, and a wholesale-retail distribution system involving a post office, a train, its tracks, and, in short, the Industrial Revolution.

That revolution came to America in the astounding memory of one man, Samuel Slater, who arrived in Philadelphia in 1789 with the plans of all Arkwright's, Crompton's, and Hargreaves's machinery in his head, put himself at the service of the rich Quaker Moses Brown, and built the first American factory at Pawtucket, Rhode Island.

The apron is trimmed with rickrack ribbon, a machine-made substitute for lace. The curtains are bordered in a variant of the egg-and-dart design that comes from Nabataea, the Biblical Edom, in Syria, a design which the architect Hiram incorporated into the entablatures of Solomon's temple—"and the chapiters upon the two pillars had pomegranates also above,

over against the belly which was by the network: and the pomegranates were two hundred in rows round about" (1 Kings 7:20) and which formed the border of the high priest's dress, a frieze of "pomegranates of blue, and of purple, and of scarlet, around about the hem thereof; and bells of gold between them round about" (Exodus 28:33).

The brass button that secures the farmer's collar is an unassertive, puritanical understatement of Matthew Boulton's eighteenth-century cut-steel button made in the factory of James Watt. His shirt button is mother-of-pearl, made by James Boepple from Mississippi fresh-water mussel shell, and his jacket button is of South American vegetable ivory passing for horn.

The farmer and his wife are attended by symbols, she by two plants on the porch, a potted geranium and sansevieria, both tropical and alien to Iowa; he by the three-tined American pitchfork whose triune shape is repeated throughout the painting, in the bib of the overalls, the windows, the faces, the siding of the house, to give it a formal organization of impeccable harmony.

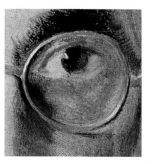

If this painting is primarily a statement about Protestant diligence on the American frontier, carrying in its style and subject a wealth of information about imported technology, psychology, and aesthetics, it still does not turn away from a pervasive cultural theme of Mediterranean origin—a tension between the growing and the ungrowing, between vegetable and mineral, organic and inorganic, wheat and iron.

Transposed back into its native geography, this icon of the lord of metals with his iron sceptre, head wreathed with glass and silver, buckled in tin and brass, and a chaste bride who has already taken on the metallic thraldom of her plight in the gold ovals of her hair and brooch, are Dis and Persephone posed in a royal portrait among the attributes of the first Mediterranean trinity, Zeus in the blue sky and lightning rod, Poseidon in the trident of the pitchfork, Hades in the metals. It is a picture of a sheaf of golden grain, female and cyclical, perennial and the mother of civilization; and of metal shaped into scythe and hoe: nature and technology, earth and farmer, man and world, and their achievement together.

(1981)

EDWARD HOPPER'S *NIGHTHAWKS*, 1942

The three men are fully clothed, long sleeves,
even hats, though it's indoors, and brightly lit,
and there's a woman. The woman is wearing
a short-sleeved red dress cut to expose her arms,
a curve of her creamy chest; she's contemplating
a cigarette in her right hand, thinking that
her companion has finally left his wife but
can she trust him? Her heavy-lidded eyes,
pouty lipsticked mouth, she has the redhead's
true pallor like skim milk, damned good-looking
and she guesses she knows it but what exactly
has it gotten her so far, and where?—he'll start
to feel guilty in a few days, she knows
the signs, an actual smell, sweaty, rancid, like
dirty socks; he'll slip away to make telephone calls
and she swears she isn't going to go through that
again, isn't going to break down crying or begging
nor is she going to scream at him, she's finished
with all that. And he's silent beside her,
not the kind to talk much but he's thinking
thank God he made the right move at last,
he's a little dazed like a man in a dream—
is this a dream?—so much that's wide, still,
mute, horizontal, and the counterman in white,
stooped as he is and unmoving, and the man
on the other stool unmoving except to sip
his coffee; but he's feeling pretty good,
it's primarily relief, this time he's sure
as hell going to make it work, he owes it to her
and to himself, Christ's sake. And she's thinking
the light in this place is too bright, probably
not very flattering, she hates it when her lipstick
wears off and her makeup gets caked, she'd like

to use a ladies' room but there isn't one here
and Jesus how long before a gas station opens?—
it's the middle of the night and she has a feeling
time is never going to budge. This time
though she isn't going to demean herself—
he starts in about his wife, his kids, how
he let them down, they trusted him and he let
them down, she'll slam out of the goddamned room
and if he calls her *Sugar* or *Baby* in that voice,
running his hands over her like he has the right,
she'll slap his face hard, *You know I hate that: Stop!*
And he'll stop. He'd better. The angrier
she gets the stiller she is, hasn't said a word
for the past ten minutes, not a strand
of her hair stirs, and it smells a little like ashes
or like the henna she uses to brighten it, but
the smell is faint or anyway, crazy for her
like he is, he doesn't notice, or mind—
burying his hot face in her neck, between her cool
breasts, or her legs—wherever she'll have him,
and whenever. She's still contemplating
the cigarette burning in her hand,
the counterman is still stooped gaping
at her, and he doesn't mind that, why not,
as long as she doesn't look back, in fact
he's thinking he's the luckiest man in the world
so why isn't he happier?

(1989)

LISTENING

If one can ascribe to a painting something like the all-encompassing memory of music, I hear the dark figure in the right margin of William Sidney Mount's *Walking the Line* (1835) listening, then finding himself in the moment this picture conveys. I enter his space, his corner, become him, as he enters the space of the painting, enters the artist's imagination, a detail appearing perhaps as an afterthought, filler, a mote in the artist's eye instinctively transferred onto the canvas, or perhaps a hidden key to the painting's meaning, prime force and mover of everything else the painter wishes to express. Perhaps both.

I'm offered an opportunity to write about any painting or painter in the collection of The Art Institute of Chicago, and I chose one of the few paintings I've never seen before. If seen, forgotten. Leafing through a handsome volume of *Master Paintings in The Art Institute of Chicago,* my only access to the collection since I'm in Maine not Chicago at the moment, I find almost no other recognizable images of people of African descent. The only other I can recall after shutting the volume, a torturer whose skin is darker than the other torturers' in Leon Golub's *Interrogation II* (1981). What I write about Mount's work is not intended as a critique or corrective of this absence. I chose my subject because I found a familiar face in a familiar situation, heard a familiar tune playing. The black boy inside and outside the central action, included and excluded by marginalization, could be me, wandering, browsing the pages of *Master Paintings.*

The scene portrayed is a tavern interior. A group of men watch a fellow in a tattered jacket, holding aloft a tankard, who performs a dance along the "line" of a floorboard. The tavern appears more rural than urban, a simple, unadorned, barnlike space hunkering around the frieze of figures. Off to one side, but around a corner from the central grouping so they may very well be unaware of his presence, a short, squat black man,

the toes of his shoes, like the dancer's, touching the edge of a board, quietly, unobtrusively observes the merriment.

The artist composed his picture as a kind of triptych: a dominant, highlighted central panel, balanced by two wings. The left-hand panel stretches outward towards the viewer and a light source exterior to the painting. A glazed earthenware pitcher, two glass bottles shelved behind it, another on the counter beside it, gleam. The right wing recedes to a shadowed alcove where the even darker mass of the negro man is planted in a corner, the area most distant from where the painting positions the viewer.

A triptych links each scene with two others, implicates time, implies narrative. *Walking the Line* suggests we read it. There's a story here, something is happening, perhaps with a beginning, middle, and end, a tale the form of triptych binds, rounds into a circle. For instance, dots of white paint indicating glints of light on glass decanters and crockery pitcher in the near left margin of the painting are echoed by dots in the eyes of the black man on the far right. Appropriately, three is a repeated compositional motif. Three stovepipe hats, three glass decanters, three chairs, three notices on the golden wall, three seated white men, three "others"—a boy, a negro, a tramp—who stand, a still-life grouping of hat, jug, long-handled axe in the foreground. Horizontally as well as vertically the painting is organized into three sections: from the top down, over a third of the space is empty; next, the busy middle with its band of human figures; then last and least, the border of plank flooring, bare as the upper third.

These clues, this patterning and organizing, lead to other levels of interpretation, other tricks through which the artist tells a story, mediates, extenuates the seemingly straightforward spontaneity of a realistic genre piece. Other paintings have come before this one and the artist situates his work in this continuum, this tradition with its customary vocabulary and syntax. Flemish golds, the Breughel-like peasant awkwardness of the dancer's posture render an aesthetic dialect for us to read. Another story and language are embodied in the black man in a corner, up against a wall, his toes exactly poised on the outer edges of a plank, echoing the dancer's toes straddling the plank upon which he "walks the line." The plump young black fellow smiles, his walking stick indicates a line dividing him from the other people in the tavern. Why is he smiling. What does he remember.

Is the white man in his poor, tattered coat a version of Samuel Dartmouth Rice, the music hall performer mired in a mediocre career until the night he borrows a negro stevedore's clothes (so the story goes) and jumps on stage mimicking a southern darky's accent and comical buck and wing. Rice became a national celebrity through his grotesque, minstrel rendition of black dance. *Jump about/wheel about/do just so/ Ebry time I wheel about/I jump Jim Crow.*

Is *Jim Crow* the tune I hear when I listen to this painting, listen to what the black boy hears.

Much of the painting's effect inheres in the mute lyricism of color. Empty space, caves, planes of color modelled, harmonized, close to monochromatic. Brown—from coffee black to muddied gray-brown to reddish-brown to sand, brass, palomino, burnished gold, pale gold—a palette in effect of African-American skin tones, the parchment upon which the story inscribes itself.

Brown rhythms. Irony and paradox. The dark excluded boy on the far side of the line who can see himself in the others' merrymaking, even though they can't see him, don't see him when they do. The brown boy dreams the scene as complexly, as poignantly, as clinically as the artist because like the artist he lives at a vast disciplined distance from what's in front of him, his internal responses conditioned to be contrapuntal, fugal, variations on unresolvable themes he can only express through a medium that is eternally suspect, not quite real, like memory, like music or words or paint.

Or is the squat, dark shape a mote in the painter's eye. Something similar to the few dots of white paint, the few dripping, bloody reds the artist perhaps could have left out of the painting, but then would have had no painting if he'd neglected to insert them. A reminder to himself, there's more to hear than meets the eye. The house of cards collapses when one card is removed. More to America than America can afford to ignore or leave out, more that returns as an afterthought even when you believed you were finished with your picture, out of harm's way, the logic and structure of the painting dense enough, complete enough to require not one more drop of pigment. Then you blink, the wet brush still in your fist, and a blank spot assails you. A rock in your eye. You blink.

Walking the Line. Twenty-five years from the date of this painting a bloody civil war, though it ultimately settles nothing about issues of race and class and commerce sparking it, will demonstrate how fine, how precarious the line really was. Look again. Listen again. Maybe every person in the tavern understands what is going to happen. Observe the frozen faces of the three seated spectators, their paleness, doll-like features. The hands of one poised to produce a clap that will shock their world into motion again. A thin snake of smoke twists from a pipe. One man seems hypnotized by the dancer's feet. Yet all three seated men, each representing a season of life, are unconnected, their stares vacant, each locked in his own solipsistic middle distance. Imminent thunder of the clap, the ominous smoke, indecipherable notices on the wall (advertising fugitive slaves, slaves for sale?), crosses on the door in the black man's niche, the white boy's otherworldly gaze. The line is thin indeed. The shadow in the corner, like Yeats' great beast slouching towards Bethlehem, will fall across this scene. Golden light of nostalgia will fade, lines dissolve, walls crumble, burn. Perhaps the black man hears martial music, fife and trumpet, the missing note of the slain drummer boy, the crippled veterans, glaze-eyed, tramping home from battle.

Is that what I hear. Is that the enigmatic spark or tear in the black boy's eye.

EXCERPT FROM *THE MAN WITH THE BLUE GUITAR*

I

The man bent over his guitar,
A shearsman of sorts. The day was green

They said, "You have a blue guitar,
You do not play things as they are."

The man replied, "Things as they are
Are changed upon the blue guitar."

And they said then, "But play, you must,
A tune beyond us, yet ourselves,

A tune upon the blue guitar
Of things exactly as they are."

II

I cannot bring a world quite round,
Although I patch it as I can.

I sing a hero's head, large eye
And bearded bronze, but not a man,

Although I patch him as I can
And reach through him almost to man.

If to serenade almost to man
Is to miss, by that, things as they are,

Say that it is the serenade
Of a man that plays a blue guitar.

III

Ah, but to play man number one,
To drive the dagger in his heart,

To lay his brain upon the board
And pick the acrid colors out,

To nail his thought across the door,
Its wings spread wide to rain and snow,

To strike his living hi and ho,
To tick it, tock it, turn it true,

To bang it from a savage blue,
Jangling the metal of the strings . . .

IV

So that's life, then: things as they are?
It picks its way on the blue guitar.

A million people on one string?
And all their manner in the thing.

And all their manner, right and wrong,
And all their manner, weak and strong?

The feelings crazily, craftily call,
Like a buzzing of flies in autumn air,

And that's life, then: things as they are,
This buzzing of the blue guitar.

V

Do not speak to us of the greatness of poetry,
Of the torches wisping in the underground,

Of the structure of vaults upon a point of light.
There are no shadows in our sun,

Day is desire and night is sleep.
There are no shadows anywhere.

The earth, for us, is flat and bare.
There are no shadows. Poetry

Exceeding music must take the place
of empty heaven and its hymns,

Ourselves in poetry must take their place,
Even in the chattering of your guitar.

VI

A tune beyond us as we are,
Yet nothing changed by the blue guitar;

Ourselves in the tune as if in space,
Yet nothing changed, except the place

Of things as they are and only the place
As you play them, on the blue guitar,

Placed, so, beyond the compass of change,
Perceived in a final atmosphere;

For a moment final, in the way
The thinking of art seems final when

The thinking of god is smoky dew.
The tune is space. The blue guitar

Becomes the place of things as they are,
A composing of senses of the guitar.

(1936)

RITA DOVE

On Ivan Albright, *Into the World There Came a Soul Called Ida, 1929–30*

 THERE CAME A SOUL

She arrived as near to virginal
as girls got in those days—i.e., young,
the requisite dewy cheek
flushed at its own daring.
He had hoped for a little more edge.
But she held the newspaper rolled like a scepter,
his advertisement turned up to prove
she was there solely at his bidding—and yet
the gold band, the photographs . . . a mother, then.

He placed her in the old garden chair,
the same one he went to evenings
when the first tug on the cord sent the bulb
swinging like the lamps in the medic's tent
over the wounded, swaddled shapes that moaned
each time the Screaming Meemies let loose,
their calculated shrieks so far away
he thought of crickets—while all around him
matted gauze and ether pricked up
an itch so bad he could hardly sketch
each clean curve of tissue opening up.
I shut my eyes, walk straight to it.
Nothing special but it's there, wicker
fraying under my calming fingers.

What if he changed the newspaper into a letter,
then ripped it up and tucked the best part
from view? How much he needed that desecrated
scrap! And the red comb snarled with a few
pale hairs for God in his infinite greed
to snatch upon like a hawk targeting a sparrow—
he couldn't say *At least I let you keep your hair*
so he kept to his task, applying paint
like a bandage to the open wound.

Pretty Ida, out to earn a penny
for her tiny brood.
He didn't mask the full lips
or the way all the niggling fears
of an adolescent century
shone through her hesitant eyes,
but he painted the room out, blackened
every casement, every canvas drying
along the wall, even the ailing coffeepot
whose dim brew she politely refused,
until she was seated
as he had been, dropped
bleak and thick,
onto the last chair in the world.

JOHN YAU
On Jasper Johns, *Corpse and Mirror II,* 1974–75

AFTER A PAINTING BY JASPER JOHNS

It was only difficult being a corpse when he began forgetting the days that preceded the change in his status. Didn't I used to look in the mirror each morning? Wasn't I once something else besides a corpse? But what did I see when I looked in the mirror?, and what does it look like when no one is in front of it? Is it a corpse of some kind?, cold and alone in the shifting light. Why do I remember these words: You cannot become someone else's mirror no matter how hard you try? I am not a corpse, he thought, I am its shadow.

A mirror is a wall you stand in front of in the morning, as well as at night before going to sleep. He thinks: If I am not a corpse, but its shadow, what did I do in the hours that fill the air between sunrise and sunset? Did I go to a room where there was no mirror of any kind? Did the others in that place think I was a corpse? Had one of them been my mirror, would I have been able to see myself as I now am? Perhaps I was a corpse before I became a shadow, a ball which never lands in the brown leather glove flapping below, like a mouth with no teeth. I remember the words, I look in the mirror, but I have no memory of what I said next.

Who do you see when you look at a corpse? I remember the mirror was turned to the wall and that the blinds were drawn. I was a cloud floating above and below a corpse striped by slats of light filtering into the hazy room; and it held my name under its tongue. A mirror is a wall we fail to look at, didn't I say that once? We think that unlike a corpse, it must show us something other than itself. I looked in a mirror and did not see anything that I knew, it was my shadow staring back at me. But a corpse, I said to my reflection, talks to itself in a language that no one else understands; it is either an idea or something that vanishes before it begins.

If a mirror has no ideas, then what does it say to us? It says: I am a corpse without a body, a body you want to inhabit, as if it is your own. It says: I mirror the world you are leaving behind, but I am not the place in which you will arrive. It says: A corpse is neither a surface nor a place. And a mirror is a thing one thinks of as both surface and a place. Is this the place, I ask, where the corpse never arrives, the place where I have never been? Or is it that both these things mirror each other by becoming more themselves?

IVAN ALBRIGHT: SELF-PORTRAITS, 1981–83

The men and women in Albright's paintings, with their wrinkles and warts, their puffy faces, swollen hands and rheumy eyes, can look like they have only barely survived a traumatic disease. But the disease is simply mortality. Albright's detailing of imperfection, even in the faces and bodies of the young, seems perversely enthusiastic. "All things are dead," he wrote. Albright sees the presence of ruin everywhere. Everything is physical, almost repulsively so: disfigured human figures. Yet he also wrote: "Life is in all things"—the gnarly unpleasant surfaces of his subjects are also a sign of experience, of bearing on one's body the evidence of having been alive. Life as damage.

Sometimes I have felt almost ashamed to want to look at Albright's works, guilty of bad manners, as though I were staring in the grocery store at a misshapen or scarred person: the pornographic fascination of what's ugly.

In 1981 Albright began a series of self-portraits on gessoed wood panels only a foot high and a little narrower than that; after he had finished eighteen, he suffered a stroke. In the hospital he finished three more before he died. The eighteen are very Albright: powerful depictions of human vulnerability, of the precariousness of consciousness itself, of the threats of bewilderment, shock, and stupor that besiege the living mind. Albright's insistently unbeautiful portrayal of the human head says that even the life in that head, the life in the mind, is material, physical, corporeal.

It was on a visit to the Art Institute in 1984 that I happened to see a few of the self-portraits for the first time, exhibited temporarily as new acquisitions. I felt I was in the presence of two different artists. One, whose celebrated technical skill and whose thousands of *things*—his paints, brushes, other materials, and all the objects he had accumulated in order to study and paint them—had been stolen from him by his infirmity. And another artist, who, having intrepidly imagined life and death in heavy and elaborately unpleasant detail, having insisted that "The body is always dead / It is an empty hulk animated by life," drew very differently when he was weak and dying: sketchily, delicately, lightly. I felt that the meaning of Albright's last three self-portraits was that, for a brief time, he had occupied a tormented and privileged place far from life and very close to death.

But it was not the death he had been implying in the technique of his earlier work—death profusely mottling and freaking and corrupting the friable body. Death's interest in the body, death's effect on the body, is no more devastating than death's stalking of the mind. Did Albright's stroke only impair his control of his hand, or did it also shift his sense of the human figure from the image of living mortality to the image of dying spirit? In the last three self-portraits the particularities of life seem irrelevant; what is dying is not detail and the material world, not appearances, not the flesh around the skull and bones, but a mind and a heart.

In the self-portrait of August 21, 1983, Albright's touch is not just weak, it's soft. His colored pencils sketch the outline of bandaged head and robed shoulders. Most of the work is in the eyes and mouth. The whiteness of the hospital surrounds and contains him—it comes *through* him. His medium is almost transparent; so is his being. His mouth is slackly open and pulled to one side, his head is set on tired, small shoulders. The eyes are looking to Albright's right, and seem to be saying much more than the mouth will ever be able to say again. They almost look pleading.

While in the hospital, Albright wrote in his notebook:

> Those approaching in twilight gloom
> Are they real these shapes coming my way
> or are they something unreal in being
> Real but in seeming to be near me
> They approach with a silence unbearable
> Struggling bodies surging ahead
> like waves in a tempest
> They engulf me with terror

Two days later, Albright drew himself again with colored pencils. He seems to be a little farther away.

The bandage on his head is clearly outlined, and his ears, and the collar of his shirt. Nothing else except his eyes has much presence. He is a seeing mind looking out from a simplified, almost transparent head. The mouth and nose are scarcely suggested. He gazes straight out this time and his eyes are dark and clouded, his right eye larger than his left, and drifting. The eyes, intense dark smudges against the white, seem about to well with tears. A person suffering quiet, unbearable harrowing.

Curators have designated the remaining self-portrait—the fullest, dated "August" by Albright—as the last of the three, but given how much more finished it is, with pastels as well as with colored pencils, it is a wonder that this work isn't earlier than the other two. If it is the last, it shows a supreme effort to produce, rather than a sketchy work, a perfected one, and a more material one, to represent one last time the physicality of existence. Against a yellow background Albright appears with a white bandage or hospital cap on his head. Head and shoulders are fully sketched, mouth and nose and ears fully realized, and the cold whiteness of the hospital cannot come through him any more. His eyes are again the focus of the self-portrait. They have a little glitter in them, they are no longer dull, but they are bleary and tired, sorrowful and emotionally vulnerable. They gaze inward.

In all three images, gone are the myriad tiny features that make up a human face. Earlier Albrights are all about the human skin, but in these self-portraits the subject has no skin. And in a sense he has no skull, either—that is, there is no attempt at the illusion of depth in the picture plane, except to a limited degree in depicting the head against the yellow background.

There are not three dimensions at this moment of life, in this foyer of death. With weak hand but potent effect Albright creates the image not of a living presence but of a powerless recollection of having lived.

He also tried to grasp with language what was happening to him. On August 31 he wrote:

> Things most important to me are lost
> And in their place rises colossal
> terror and fear and nights of eternal length
> Bring uncalled-for colors and sounds
> And mirrors appear that were not
> there before and half alive
> They slip about the room waist high

This is an eerie and startling poetic fragment, in which the low gliding mirrors, like live creatures of the silent visual world, threaten the dying man. Having worked, presumably, from a mirror, as well as photographs, the self-portraitist is surrounded now by the mocking device of his artistic project, which will reflect nothing when he is dead. Death is no longer a corruption, a physical claim on even the perfect bodies of youth; it no longer has to do with the physical. It is a quiet look of fear and a soft cry that cannot be made loud enough to be heard.

Now the issue was not corruption or decay at all, nor even the material world to which paints and wood panels and the body belong, but the realm of what is intended, wanted, regretted, dreamed, felt. Who but the lifelong painter of the density, solidity, and decay of the flesh could have painted at the very last moment so astonishing a portrait of the spirit?

BLAISE CENDRARS
On Robert Delaunay, *Champs de Mars: The Red Tower,* 1911

THE EIFFEL TOWER

For Madame Sonia Delaunay

. . . In the years 1910, 1911, Robert Delaunay and I were perhaps the only ones in Paris talking about machines and art and with a vague awareness of the great transformation of the modern world.

At that time, I was working in Chartres, with B . . . , on the perfecting of his plane with variable angles of incidence, and Robert, who had worked for a time as journeyman mechanic, in some artisan locksmith's shop, was prowling, in a blue coat, around the Eiffel Tower.

One day, as I was coming back from Chartres, I fell out of the car at the exit of the Parc du Saint-Cloud and broke my leg. I was carried to the nearest hotel, the Hôtel de Palais, kept by Alexandre Dumas and his sons. I stayed there, in that hotel bed, for twenty-eight days, lying on my back with a weight pulling on my leg. I had had the bed pushed against the window. Thus, every morning, when the boy brought me my breakfast, threw open the shutters, and opened the window wide, I had the impression he was bringing me Paris on his tray. I could see, through the window, the Eiffel Tower like a clear flask of water, the domes of the Invalides and the Panthéon like a teapot and a sugar bowl, and Sacré-Cœur, white and pink, like a candy. Delaunay came almost every day to keep me company. He was always haunted by the Tower and the view from my window attracted him strongly. He would often sketch or bring his box of colors.

It was thus I was able to be present at an unforgettable drama: the struggle of an artist with a subject so new that he didn't know how to capture it, to subdue it. I have never seen a man struggle and defend himself so, except perhaps the mortally wounded men abandoned on the field of battle who, after two or three days of superhuman efforts, would finally quiet

down and return to the night. But he, Delaunay, remained victor.

• • •

And now, think of my hotel window opening onto Paris. It was the subject of all his preoccupations, a ready-made painting which had to be interpreted, constructed, painted, created, expressed. And that was quite difficult. In that year, 1911, Delaunay painted, I believe, fifty-one canvases of the Eiffel Tower before succeeding.

As soon as I could go out, I went with Delaunay to see the Tower. Here is our trip around and in the Tower.

No art formula known until then could make the pretense of resolving plastically the problem of the Eiffel Tower. Realism made it smaller; the old laws of Italian perspective made it look thinner. The Tower rose above Paris, as slender as a hat pin. When we walked away from it, it dominated Paris, stiff and perpendicular; when we approached it, it bowed and leaned out over us. Seen from the first platform, it wound like a corkscrew, and seen from the top, it collapsed under its own weight, its legs spread out, its neck sunk in. Delaunay also wanted to depict Paris around it, to situate it. We tried all points of view, we looked at it from all angles, from all sides, and its sharpest profile is the one you can see from the Passy footbridge. And those thousands of tons of iron, those 35 million bolts, those 300 meters high of interlaced girders and beams, those four arcs with a spread of 100 meters, all that jellylike mass flirted with us. On certain spring days it was supple and laughing and opened its parasol of clouds under our very nose. On certain stormy days it sulked, sour and ungracious; it seemed cold. At midnight we ceased to exist, all its fires were for New York with whom it was already flirting then; and at noon it gave the time

to ships on the high seas. It taught me the Morse code which allows me today to understand radio messages. And as we were prowling around it, we discovered that it exerted a singular attraction for a host of people. Lovers climbed a hundred, two hundred meters over Paris to be alone; couples on their honeymoon came from the provinces or from abroad to visit it; one day we met a boy of fifteen who had traveled from Düsseldorf to Paris, on foot, just to see it. The first planes turned about it and said hello, Santos-Dumont had already taken it for his destination at the time of his memorable dirigible flight, as the Germans were to take it for their target during the war, a symbolic and not a strategic target, and I assure you that he wouldn't have hit it because the Parisians would have killed themselves for it, and Gallieni had decided to blow it up, our own Tower!

So many points of view to treat the problem of the Eiffel Tower. But Delaunay wanted to interpret it plastically. He finally succeeded with the famous canvas that everybody knows. He took the Tower apart to make it fit into his frame, he truncated it, and bent it to give it 300 meters of dizzying height, he adopted 10 points of view, 15 perspectives, so that one part is seen from below, another from above, the houses surrounding it are taken from the right, from the left, bird's-eye view, level with the ground. . . .

(1924)

CHARLES SHEELER'S *THE ARTIST LOOKS AT NATURE* (1943)

He paints what he sees, seeing what he paints.

What our eye takes from the scene of his eye
Taking what it does from his photograph,
Taken itself in, and of, the room, takes
Visual counsel from another kind
Of otherness: the eyeing mind and the
Reminded eye are all their own *plein-air.*

It is all so natural: no magic
Of word becoming unlikely image
Here puzzles the very clarity of
Everything in which it all shapes up (like
Magritte's locomotive, say, out of scale,
Emerging from the empty fireplace
As from some sort of invisible, short
Tunnel through third-dimensionality,
Running on time—but not on tracks—in space,
We had been looking at a while ago.)

No. The puzzle here is only the one
Always lurking on the flip side of the
Flat, deep *there* of our gaze: the thingness
Of the picture, the so pictorial
Nature of the thing, the indoors the eye
Is always in whatever the outdoors,
The *camera chiara* of whatever room—
Indoors, outdoors, virtual space, the flat
Or roughened pleasant lands of picture-plane
Unshadowed by any modelling, on
(And, thereby, *in*) which all the forms can live
And move and have their sort of being—that
Painting can provide.

                        Yes, an easy joke
Is still there to read: the large landscape of
The *Campagna* being painted away
At in the studio in Rome, or at
Home in the North, is no more or less done
Dal Vero—from nature—than what Sheeler's
Sheeler is doing in this place. (A man's
Studio is his castle, I suppose,
And real artists are always working from
The battlements, even when the easel's
Base implies a spatial pun upon the
Carpet of lawn both flush with and below
The parapet.) The painter's place makes up
Its own space, and the world drops down, drops up
And back away from it in the crazy
Almost Sienese perspective that the
Solid orthogonals of the painted
Interior with Stove have made mock of.

We contemplate, in the painted painting
So tonal it recalls a photograph,
The high, dark stovepipe pointing into as
Much of an upward as the easel's post—
High in a green sea of grassy air, at
One less remove here from the Palpable—
To which it alludes: the artist at work
Overlooks not a forest of symbols
But a field of signs. And what he paints are
Signs—as if road-signs pointing *in* or *out*—
Within or quite beyond ourselves—rather
Than *this way to Wimberby, three more miles.*
Yet the ambitious paintings—histories,
The loves of Jove, scenes from the life of Christ,
Portraits, still-lives, pictures of forms and marks
And voids, maps of virtual space, glimpses
Of rooms and, of course, landscapes: no matter
How noble or base fashion may rank them
Are all—in our fashionable patter—
Painted signs (and works by masters are—in
An old-fashioned patter—signed all over).
But then, the very work of painting signs

Itself, the shadow of the act falling
Across the surface of the fictive veil
That gives our eyes access to the room and
Prevents our touch—*Don't even think of it!*—
From verifying its tall tale of depth:
That alien form on the pictured picture?
—The shadow of the hand of the mind's eye.

The eye does its own kind of painting first:
(In vivid illustration of this, see
Morandi painting the surfaces of
His pots, then placing them in a still-life
Set-up and painting them—in another
Sense—again—painting as making and as
Representing.) And so with "landscape": a scene,
A scene as seen, a painting of just that.

Why not paint painting—painting itself—then?
The Odyssey is as natural, as
Much part of what's out there, as the profound
Aegean Sea is; so is Sheeler's picture
Done from the natural, the photograph:
So when he comes at length its parts to frame
Nature and painting are to him the same.

The *nature* of painting? Its inner truth
Is the namesake of its totality
Of objects: true to art is true to both.
Our marks are sounded in a sea of talk:
Thus, perhaps, we shorten pencil into
Pen and figuratively illustrate
Sheeler's bright aphoristical remarks
On the nature of representation
And the representation of nature.

The painting says: *Figure it out yourself.*

GERALD STERN
On Chaim Soutine, *Dead Fowl,* 1926

THE JEW AND THE ROOSTER ARE ONE

After fighting with his dead brothers and his dead sisters
he chose to paint the dead rooster of his youth,
thinking God wouldn't mind a rooster, would he?—or thinking
a rooster would look good in a green armchair
with flecks of blood on his breast and thighs, his wings
resting a little, their delicate bones exposed, a
few of the plumes in blue against the yellow
naked body, all of *those* feathers plucked
as if by a learned butcher, and yet the head
hanging down, the comb disgraced, the mouth
open as if for screaming, the right front chair leg,
seen from a certain angle, either a weapon
or a strong right arm, a screaming arm, the arm
of an agitator; and yet at the same time the chair
as debonair as any, the brown mahogany
polished, the carving nineteenth century, the velvet
green, an old velour, as if to match
the plumes a little, a blue with a green. No rabbi
was present, this he knew, and no dead butcher
had ever been there with his burnished knife
and his bucket of sand; this was the angry rooster
that strutted from one small house to another, that scratched
among the rhubarb, he is the one who stopped
as if he were thinking, he is upside down now
and plucked. It looks as if his eye can hardly
contain that much of sorrow, as if it wanted
to disappear, and it looks as if his legs
were almost helpless, and though his body was huge
compared to the armchair, it was only more
horrible that way, and though his wings were lifted
it wasn't for soaring, it was more for bedragglement
and degradation. Whatever else there was
of memory there had to be revenge there,

even revenge on himself, for he had to be
the rooster, though that was easy, he was the armchair
too, and he was the butcher, it was a way
to understand, there couldn't be another, he had to
paint like that, he had to scrape the skin
and put the blotches on, and though it was
grotesque to put a dead rooster in an armchair
his table could have been full, or he just liked
the arrangement, or he was good at painting a chair
and it was done first—although I doubt it—or someone
brought him the bird—a kind of gift—for food was
cheap then, and roosters were easy to cook; but it was
more than anything else a kind of Tartar,
a kind of Jew, he was painting, something
that moved from Asia to Europe, something furious,
ill and dreamy, something that stood in the mud
beside a large wooden building and stared at a cloud,
it was so deep in thought, and it had tears
in a way, there was no getting around that kind
of thinking even if he stood in the middle of the room
holding his paintbrush like a thumb at arm's length
closing one of his eyes he still was standing
in the mud shrieking, he still was dying for corn,
he still was golden underneath his feathers
with freckles of blood, for he was a ripped-open Jew,
and organs all on show, the gizzard, the liver,
for he was a bleeding Tartar, and he was a Frenchman
dying on the way to Paris and he was
tethered to a table, he was slaughtered.

SUSAN STEWART
On Francis Bacon, *Figure with Meat*, 1954

EXPLOSION AT SAN GIOVANNI IN LATERANO, SUMMER 1993: NOTES ON FRANCIS BACON'S *FIGURE WITH MEAT*

Omnium urbis et orbis . . .
The writer's habit is overdetermination; the painter's, obsession.

———

Francis Bacon felt by 1962 that the more than twenty-five paintings based upon Velázquez's *Portrait of Pope Innocent X* and contemporary photographs of Pius XII he had completed ten years or so before were "silly" and he regretted doing them. It was his practice, throughout the 1950s and 1960s, to destroy much of his work. But he also explained that he had been obsessed, not with the Velázquez original at the Galleria Doria Pamphili —which he, though in Rome, in fact had never gone to see— but with reproduction after reproduction of the painting.

———

In The Art Institute of Chicago's 1954 *Figure with Meat* his obsession is coming to a close and the elements of the Pope series—the monochromatic background; the vitrine-like structure with its shifting gestalt between solid and plane, inside and outside; the Velázquez reference—are urgently yoked to a self-citation: his *Painting* of 1946 with its opened carcass of meat. And the elements of Bacon's lifelong study of figuration— the head as the locus of the expression of emotion; animal motion and rest; gesture, cry, and action in a frame of contingent circumstances—seem to lie in wait here and open to view.

———

When Pope John Paul II visited the site of the explosion he said that one must pity the miserable creatures who had brought it about.

———

" . . . when I made the Pope screaming, I didn't want to do it in the way that I did it—I wanted to make the mouth, with the beauty of its color and everything, look like one of the sunsets or something of Monet . . ."

———

In Soutine's paintings of meat, the pity for an animal and the pity for the human mind which cannot know its animal nature are synonymous. Bacon saw the crucifixion (picturing Cimabue's strung-up Christ or Caravaggio's inverted Saint Peter) as continuous with butchery, "a way of behavior to another."

———

Everything hinges on the particular, immediate, acknowledgment of death, which for Bacon was expressed in the animal fear of eyes and mouth. Symmetry of the carcass and the crucifixion as the symmetry between god and animal or the reciprocity of two players in a game.

———

The image of Eisenstein's screaming nanny is etched onto the face of the Velázquez Pope; the balled fists of an executed man have taken the place of Innocent's lightly resting hands, the left holding a piece of paper, the right protruding the insignia of the ring.

———

The painting as rebus: the obsession with an image as the obsession with a message. *Slaughter/massacre/innocent/sacre*: the obsession with a message as the obsession with an image— a source of the screaming mouth in Bacon's work can be seen in Poussin's *The Massacre of the Innocents* at Chantilly.

———

In the Doria-Pamphili, in the same alcove and immediately at a right angle to the Velázquez, is Bernini's portrait bust of Innocent X. Carved from life: the fragility of the facial bones, the soft spread of the cloth, the eyes looking off into the distance, the shadows on the forehead and eyes, one button slightly undone, the marble in many gradations of polish—so thin at

the ear that the stone is transparent. Bernini's proficient eagerness to please as inseparable from the narcissism of absolute skill.

_____

(But Innocent had turned to Borromini for the restoration of San Giovanni in Laterano; his rigorous logic of light and darkness; his laurel-leaves, palm leaves, and pomegranates; all "nervous," "crisp," and fundamental. Just as in Sant'Agnese fuori le Mura an ancient torso was incorporated into a statue of Sant'Agnese, Borromini took fragments of the tombs from the old basilica and put them into new monuments. Manslaughter, 1649: when he found a man tampering with the stonework of the basilica, Borromini and his helpers beat him to death. Innocent intervened to save them from punishment. Geometry as redemption from the clumsy violence of life—Borromini, too, turned against himself.)

_____

In Bacon destruction stems from irrevocability—the irrevocability of time. The economy of his practice demands that the painting not go beyond a certain point or the work is lost; in this economy, excess requires—demands—destruction. To paint beyond the work is to introduce the tyranny of a will which would push the work over into stasis and death. Hence the aleatory as sacred: in reverence the painter maintains the spinning theater of action, the great wheel driven by fate and contingency which carries him beyond the merely articulate and intelligible.

_____

The Velázquez portrait: the florid face below the red satin pileolus and above the red satin mozzetta, the lace rochet with punto avorio edging, the red velvet _sedia_ with its gold banding and gold finials, the whole enveloped in a heavy red drapery stained by the _sedia_'s tapered shadow. Bacon will take the red from the figure and displace it to the carcass; he will lift the shadow's joint-like shape and splay it symmetrically behind the figure.

_____

Velázquez returned the gold chain the Pope had offered as a prize for the portrait. He wrote on the sheet of paper, held between the thumb and forefinger of the Pope's left hand:

Alla San(ta) de N(ro) Sig(re) / Innocencio X(o) / Per / Diego de Silva / Velázquez de la Ca / mera di S.M(ta) Catt(ca).

_____

Haunted by an image, obsessed by a face. For Velázquez, the object is to paint seeing, for Bacon, the "deep game" of the feeling of life.

_____

Radiographs of artworks and the body. These two uses of the technology appear incongruously in tandem as the turning of the inside out: the radiograph of the painting reveals layers of intentional actions, the history of the painter's will; the radiograph of the body fragments, partitions, pinpoints, frames, and marks the site of decay and dissolution. Bacon's text here is K. C. Clark's 1929 _Positioning in Radiography_. In _Figure with Meat_ the radiographic arrow points to the most interior space of the slaughtered body, away from the pope who seems to spill forward, as if the _sedia_ had been ejected. Despite the influence of Titian's veiling, Bacon's scoured surfaces and striations echo with uncanny precision, as if his portraits were _underneath_ the Baroque works, radiographs of the Velázquez. In this, and not in any gesture toward immortality, the painter has turned against time.

_____

Meaning as a coming forward.

_____

Destruction in the basilica of San Giovanni in Laterano: c. 455, 896, 1308, 1360, 1993.

_____

There is no natural history of terror.

LOOKING AT THE UNBEARABLE

First of all, it's a series—though not a narrative. A sequence (of images, and their captions) to be read. In its original state, something like a book: loose pages, a portfolio. In reproduction, invariably a book.

Easy to imagine more plates. Indeed, to the eighty published in the first edition of 1863, in Madrid by the Royal Academy of San Fernando, later editions invariably include at least two more plates, clearly intended for the series but which were rediscovered after 1863.

Easy to imagine fewer plates, too. How few? How do they kill thee? Let me count the ways.

Would one image be enough? (*The Disaster of War?*) No.

• • •

How to look at, how to read, the unbearable?

The problem is how not to avert one's glance. How not to give way to the impulse to stop looking.

The problem is despair. For it is not simply that this happened: Zaragoza, Chinchón, Madrid (1808–13). It *is* happening: Vucovar, Mostar, Srebrenica, Stupni Do, Sarajevo (1991–).

What to do with the knowledge communicated, shared by these images. Emerson wrote: "He has seen but half the universe who has never been shown the house of pain." It seems optimistic now to think that the house of pain describes no more than half the universe.

• • •

The images are relentless, unforgiving. That is, they do not forgive us—who are merely being shown, but do not live in the house of pain. The images tell us we have no right not to pay attention to the crimes of this order which are taking place right now. And the captions—mingling the voices of the murderers, who think of themselves as warriors, and the lamenting artist-witness—mutter and wail.

Although Goya himself may not have written the captions (anyway, they're not in his hand), it's thought that whoever did them took the phrases from the artist's notes.

They are meant—images and captions—to awaken, shock, rend. No reproduction in a book comes close in sheer unbearableness to the impact these images have in the original 1863 edition. Here in the words of some of the captions is what they show:

One cannot look at this.
This is bad.
This is how it happened.
This always happens.
There is no one to help them.
With or without reason.
He defends himself well.
He deserved it.
Bury them and keep quiet.
There was nothing to be done and he died.
What madness!
This is too much!
Why?
Nobody knows why.
Not in this case either.
This is worse.
Barbarians!
This is the absolute worst!
It will be the same.
All this and more.
The same thing elsewhere.
Perhaps they are of another breed.

I saw it.
And this too.
Truth has died.
This is the truth.

No se puede mirar. / Esto es malo. / Así sucedió. / Siempre sucede. / No hay quien los socorra. / Con razon ó sin ella. / Se defiende bien. / Lo merecia. / Enterrar y callar. / Espiró sin remedio. / Que locura! / Fuerte cosa es! / Por qué? / No se puede saber por qué. / Tampoco. / Esto es peor. / Bárbaros! / Esto es lo peor! / Será lo mismo. / Tanto y mas. / Lo mismo en otras partes. / Si son de otro linage. / Yo lo vi. / Y esto tambien. / Murió la verdad. / Esto es lo verdadero.

No hay quien los socorra.

Qué hai que hacer mas?

30

Estragos de la guerra

35

Si son de otro linage.

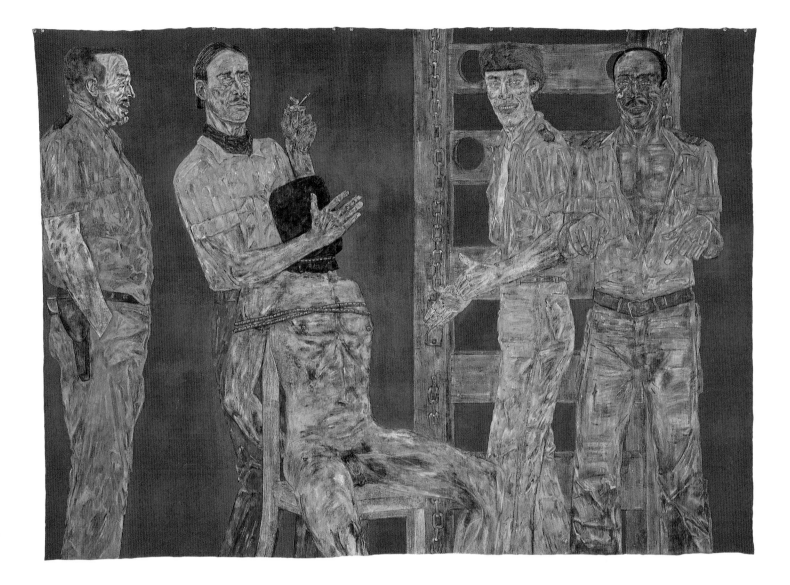

INTERROGATION II: AFTER THE PAINTING BY LEON GOLUB

1.

There will always be an issue: doctrine, dogma, differences of
      conscience, politics or creed.
There will always be a reason: heresy, rebellion, dissidence,
      inadequate conviction or compliance.

There will always be the person to command it: president or
      king, dictator or chief of staff,
and the priest or parson to anoint it, consecrate it, bless it,
      ground its logic in the sacred.

There will always be the victim: trembling, fainting, fearful,
      abducted, bound and brought here;
there will always be the order, and the brutes, thugs, reptiles,
      scum, to carry out the order.

There will always be the room, the chair, the room whose walls
      are blood, the chair of shame.
There will always be the body, hooded, helpless; and the soul
      within, trembling, fearful, shamed.

2.

If I am here, hooded, helpless,
within these walls of blood,

upon this chair of shame,
something had to think me here.

I lived within my life,
I only thought my life,

I was stolen from it:
something *thought* me from it.

If something thought me,
there had to be a mind,

and if there was a mind,
it had to be contained, revealed,

as I thought mine was contained,
within a strip of temporal being.

If it was another mind,
like mine, that thought

and bound and brought me here,
some other consciousness

within its strip of being,
didn't it, that bit of being,

have to feel as I must feel
the nothingness against it,

the nothingness encroaching
on the rind of temporality,

the strand of actuality,
in which it is revealed?

Wasn't it afraid
to jeopardize the sensitivity

with which it knows itself,
with which it senses being

trembling upon nothingness,
struggling against nothingness,

with which it holds away
the nothingness within itself

which seems to strive to join
into that greater void?

When it stole me from my life,
abducted me and bound me,

wouldn't it have felt itself
being lost within the void

of nothingness within it?
Wasn't it afraid?

3.

Why are you crying?
Nothing is happening.

No one is being tortured,
no one beaten.

Why are you crying?
Nothing is happening.

No one's genitals nails spine
crushed torn out shattered.

No one's eardrums burst with fists,
no one's brain burst with bludgeons.

Why are you crying?
Nothing is happening.

No one's bones unsocketed
fractured leaching marrow.

No one flayed, flogged, maimed,
seared with torches,

set afire racked
shot electrocuted hung.

Why are you crying?
Nothing is happening.

There is only a chair,
a room, a ladder,

flesh indelibly marked
with pain and shame.

Why are you crying?
Nothing is happening.

4.

The human soul, the soul
we share, the single soul,

that by definition
which is our essential being,

is composed of other souls,
inhabited by other beings:

thus its undeniable power,
its purity, its vision,

thus its multiplicity
in singularity.

I understand the composition
of the soul, its communality,

but must I share my soul
with brutes and reptiles,

must I share my being,
vision, purity with scum?

Impossible that in the soul
the human species

should be represented
as these brutes and thugs;

mortal substance
bodied as these reptiles.

Soul would loathe itself,
detest its very substance,

huddle in its lurk of essence
howling out its grief

of temporality, snarling out
its rage of mutability,

rather than be represented
by these beasts of prey.

The human soul is being
devoured by beasts of prey.

The human soul is prey.

5.

I didn't know the ladder to divinity on which were dreamed ascending and
        descending angels,
on which sodden spirit was supposed to rarify and rise, had become an
        instrument of torment,
wrist-holes punctured in its rungs, chains to hold the helpless body
        hammered in its uprights.

I didn't know how incidental life can seem beside such implements of
        pain and degradation;
neither did I know, though, how much presence can be manifested in the
        hooded, helpless body:
brutalized and bound, sinews, muscles, skin, still are lit with grace and
        pride and hope.

We cry from shame, because the body and the soul within are mocked,
        displayed, and shamed.
There will always be a reason, there will always be a victim, rooms of
        blood, chairs of pain.
But will there be the presence, grace and hope and pride enduring past
        the pain and shame?

STANLEY KUNITZ
On Philip Guston, *Green Sea*, 1976

 THE SEA, THAT HAS NO ENDING

"Green Sea is one of a series of paintings [Philip] Guston did in 1976 featuring a tangle of disembodied legs, bent at the knees and wearing flat, ungainly shoes, grouped on the horizon of a deep green sea against a salmon-colored backdrop. . . . Its meaning eludes us."　　　　　—descriptive note, *Master Paintings in The Art Institute of Chicago.*

Who are we? Why are we here,
huddled on this desolate shore,
so curiously chopped and joined?—
broken totems, a scruffy tribe!
How many years have passed
since we owned keys to a door,
had friends, walked down familiar streets
and answered to a name? We try
not to remember the places
where we left pieces of ourselves
along the way, whether in ditches
at the side of foreign roads
or under signs that spell "For Hire"
or naked between the sheets in cheap
motels. Does anybody care?
All the villagers have fled
from the sorry sight of us.
Once we had faith that the Master,
whose invisible presence fills the air,
watching us day and night, would hear
our cries and prove compassionate,
but we are baffled by his words
even more than by his silences.
When we complain of the fierce sun
and the blisters popping in our skin,
he turns our suffering against us:
A great wound, one you could claim
your very own, might have saved you.

Instead you let others do you in
with their small knives.
What is to become of us?
The sea, that has no ending,
is lapping at our feet.
How we long for the cleansing waters
to rise and cover us forever!
But he who reads our secret thoughts
rebukes us, saying: *You cannot hope*
to be restored unless you dare
to plunge head-down into the mystery
and there confront the beasts
that prowl on the ocean floor.
"Sacred monsters" is what he calls them.
If only we had strength enough
or nerve for a grand heroic action.
Habit has made it easier for us
to wait for the blessing of the tide.
It's really strange how much we miss
those people who came to gape and jeer;
we'd welcome their return, for company.
Why is the Master knocking at our ears,
demanding immediate attention?
In the acid of his voice we sense
the horns swelling at his temples
and little drops of spittle
bubbling at the corners of his mouth.
This is not an exhibition, he storms,
it's a life!

THE WORK OF THE WORLD

We knew all along this was coming:

The collapse of civilization, the massive nervous break-down of a social world smothering in its own contradictions and endless conflicts, the inevitable and long-promised destruc-tion of everything we hold dear—all of it gone, vanished, bur-ied like Pompeii under shards of dusty rubble and mounds of brown sod. How did that Chinese saying go? "A thousand years a city, a thousand years a forest."

For weeks I wandered, dazed and shaken, through this surreal wasteland—the planet's scorched, quiet capitals, along the unpopulated shores by her polluted seas, beneath petroleum-stained skies—and found myself at this colony, a black man barefoot and shirtless, among other survivors of the world's end, the cyclical Cataclysm, the recurrent collapse of each and every fragile, created thing. We work in an hour suspended outside time (for like all concepts, that of historical time lies buried in ruin too)—just a heartbeat after dancing Shiva has once again destroyed the world, all names and forms (*maya*), in order to balance things out, and just a heartbeat before he strikes the drum to signal it is necessary to begin the laborious process of building anew: the reinvention of lan-guages, manipulation of Nature, and conjuring of ephemeral products from the earth, and for no purpose other than to encourage beauty's efflorescence and the eruption of forms in which the divine spirit may dwell and take delight.

And of course everyone gathered here, regardless of their race or gender or religion, is crucial to that process. Is the rhythm of rising and falling away. I do not know their real names. Nor do they know mine. We have forgotten them. We change names as we change chores—or workclothes. Today my brown friend with his head down is simply called Shoveler. The woman in the red dress near me says her name is Digger. I am called Mover. The differences—the false dualisms—that divided us so badly before and led to the world's wreckage have disappeared. Like a dream, they can hardly be remem-bered. Nothing concerns us now except the question of who is willing to work. To create. To put his tired shoulder to the wheel, her parched hands on the wheelbarrow, our jobs and lives being interchangeable now—all have two good hands, two good arms, and a common goal: this thousand-year task of pulling a world phoenix-like from the ashes, reclaiming it from the forest.

But we wonder: What was the Old World about? Why the anger, wars, hatreds, petty bickering, and insignificant battles over things we should have known we could never keep for long, including life itself? In the aftermath of smash-up, in this debris where no telephone rings, no television's pale light flick-ers through the front windows of homes in the evening, and no newspaper's glaring headlines manufacture history—here nothing matters save stoking the fire that converts into plumes of white smoke the last vestiges of the Old World; cutting and carrying stone slabs; raising a haven for humanity's future in the distance; and reinforcing the earthen dais on which rests the shattered, scarred yet persisting rock that symbolizes the hope our offspring will sojourn on through time after we are gone.

After hours of hauling stones to the scaffold I am sticky with sweat and I ache in my joints. I decide to rest, joining my thirteen brothers and sisters in a circle at the base of the rock. Here will be the new city's center, one our children or grand-children may see in its glory, though most likely none of us will live that long. It goes without saying that we are a colony by accident—but a community, *satsang,* just the same. The man who a moment before struggled behind a green wheelbarrow now hands each of us a wedge of cheese and crusty chunk of bread from a sack. We share the last bottle of Coca-Cola in the

world, handing it to the person at our right after the most parsimonious of sips. Below us the forest darkens and fills with the sound of insects as light drains from the sky, leaving just the dancing, strange brilliance of the fire at twilight. No one speaks. In the wake of world's end words echo loudly against the backdrop of the Void's silence; each is energy unleashed— sacred—and so we use words sparingly. If I require a tool I need only say, "Hammer"; if my sister needs aid clearing albumen-white bones off the rock, all she need say is, "Help." And so it is best now to be silent as we rest and eat, to listen to the new world that we, like midwives, are easing from wreckage's womb.

A few of us watch the flames, fascinated by the rise of each brilliant, fugitive spark, so heartbreakingly brilliant and individual, but only for a second, for suddenly the blazing particles are gone, folded back into darkness—just as impermanent, we know, as the scaffold into which we pour every iota of our lives, labor, and love. Looking into the fire-lit faces across the circle, we wonder: Is one flickerflash instant of beauty worth our lives? Although unspoken, the answer is clear.

An instant might as well be centuries.

On Giorgio de Chirico, *The Philosopher's Conquest*, 1914

THE PHILOSOPHER'S CONQUEST

This melancholy moment will remain,
So, too, the oracle behind the gate,
And always the tower, the boat, the distant train.

Somewhere to the south a duke is slain,
A war is won. Here, it is too late.
This melancholy moment will remain.

Here, an autumn evening without rain,
Two artichokes abandoned on a crate,
And always the tower, the boat, the distant train.

Is this another scene of childhood pain?
Why do the clockhands say 1:28?
This melancholy moment will remain.

The green and yellow light of love's domain
Falls upon the joylessness of fate,
And always the tower, the boat, the distant train.

The things our vision wills us to contain—
The life of objects, their unbearable weight.
This melancholy moment will remain,
And always the tower, the boat, the distant train.

PHILIP LEVINE
On Lyonel Feininger, *Carnival in Arcueil,* 1911

A GLASS OF SEA WATER OR A PINCH OF SALT

In the city at the end of the world
there are no children, for the children
have all grown, some up to the height
of houses, while others are no taller
than their shoes and go about in coats
woven of fur. The houses, which yellow
in the sulfurous air, ignore their roomers
parading the cobbled streets at all hours.

If the world reaches from the clouds above
to the stones below, why does my father
trumpet his sorrows through the narrow lanes?
Is he calling out to me? I'm nothing,
a glass of sea water or a pinch of salt,
not even a shadow caught in the blind eyes
of the eleven irregular windows
that stare out at the August spectacle.

He wears a tall hat, my father, a short
but sturdy jacket, and bright green trousers;
he should be comfortable in this weather
with a breeze from the sea blowing the clouds
out of the eye of the sun. Does he hear
a storm gathering above the viaduct
on this afternoon of carnival?
Does he fear for the child he's never had?

In the city at the end of the world
everyone goes about in finery.
Our mothers flash their shoulders and breasts;
at all hours our fathers make their music,
the long moaning notes of the sea at rest.
Beyond the viaduct, I could be the sea spume
riding toward shore, I could be the hum
of the clouds at play, if only there were time.

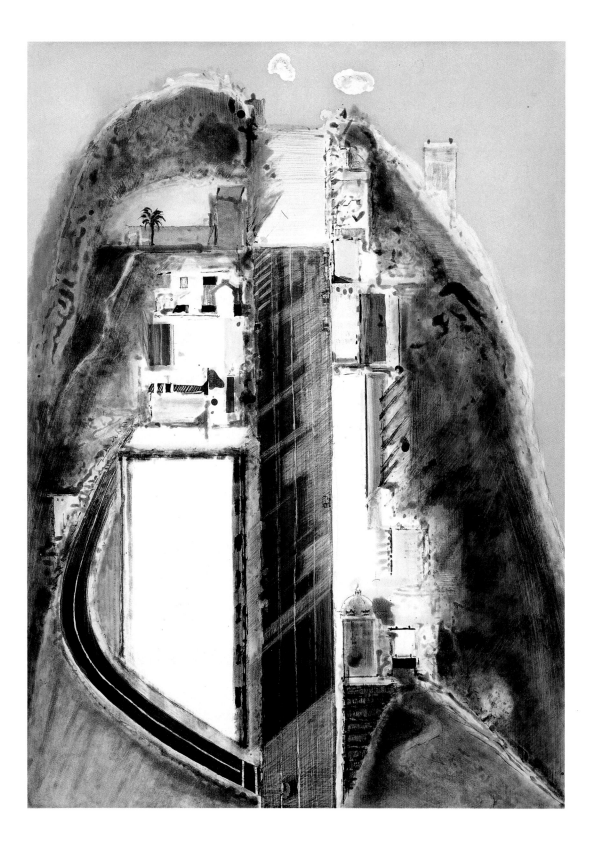

SHELBY HEARON
On Wayne Thiebaud, *Steep Street*, 1989

WAYNE THIEBAUD'S *STEEP STREET:* 1989

When I first saw Wayne Thiebaud's colored print *Steep Street,* I thought: that's the street where I live. I knew him as the painter of rows of bows, cakes on plates, slices of pies—made objects in bright primary colors which stayed where they were put. No desserts half-eaten and half-digested, no ties hanging askew or coming apart at the seams. Orderly paintings which spoke to me of the writer's need for a safe world where rules reign and gravity holds. Then here was this brave picture of a whole hill: apartments, traffic, tracks, earth, sliced like a melon down the middle with an arrow-straight street. An entire San Francisco hillside contained beneath a mellow mauve sky. With nothing falling off it, no wrecks, no urban rot, no milling mobs. And yet, what daring, a live tree, right there, risking insects and seasons, birds and squirrels. It took my breath away.

And the yellow light settling on the hill an added optimism —not a sunflower, late afternoon, school-bus yellow, but a morning, butter, and daylilies-in-the-windowsill yellow. Later, I found other Thiebaud pictures as bold: "Valley Farm, 1991," with a lone tree jutting out into a citron sunlight on a country hill, an old farmhouse, a stalwart cow guarding a rounded pond; "Apartment Hill, 1980," with not one but three trees, both hill and towering building against a custard sky. And— full-throttle bravery—the brilliant "Palm Road, 1990," with eighteen palms casting eighteen shadows on a lemon-yellow ground beneath a skyblue sky.

Other handworked versions of this print, kissing cousins, rouse different feelings. One, the colors more intense, the sur-face glossed, seems the glass mountain which the prince rode up on his white horse to take the three oranges from the prin-cess's lap. Another, darker, more intricate, calls to mind a re-writing of Scripture: Steep is the street and narrow is the way that leadeth into life and few there are who find it.

Now I'm waiting for the artist to paint the whole earth. I want a Thiebaud planet, blue and green, red and purple, wide waters and massed lands. I want a possible visual/fictional world set spinning in an egg-yolk universe. I want the surety of space itself contained.

MINA LOY
On Constantin Brancusi, *Golden Bird,* 1919/20

BRANCUSI'S *GOLDEN BIRD*

The toy
becomes the aesthetic archetype

As if
some patient peasant God
had rubbed and rubbed
the Alpha and Omega
of Form
into a lump of metal

A naked orientation
unwinged unplumed
—the ultimate rhythm
has lopped the extremities
of crest and claw
from
the nucleus flight

The absolute act
of art
conformed
to continent sculpture
—bare as the brow of Osiris—
This breast of revelation

An incandescent curve
licked by chromatic flames
in labyrinths of reflections

This gong
of polished hyperaesthesia
shrills with brass
as the aggressive light
strikes
its significance

The immaculate
conception
of the inaudible bird
occurs
in gorgeous reticence . . .

(1922)

110

THOMAS EAKINS, "STUDY FOR *WILLIAM RUSH CARVING HIS ALLEGORICAL FIGURE OF THE SCHUYLKILL RIVER*"

William Rush was a potent personal symbol for Thomas Eakins, though no artists might seem less similar. Rush (1756–1833) was a Pennsylvania artisan, a carver of ships' scrolls and figure-heads, who became a classical sculptor in wood (which he painted white, to look like marble). Eakins (1844–1916) was a professional painter, academically trained, devoted to a non-classical form of realism. Rush created his major works for public places—theaters, fountains, patriotic monuments. Eakins was a painter of privacies.

But Rush had made his way in revolutionary America with a stubborn genius that somehow fired Eakins's imagination. The painter did extensive research on the sculptor, which resulted in three major paintings with the same subject—Rush sculpting, from a live model, his fountain statue of a nymph representing a personification of the Schuylkill River. It is the first painting (1877), in the Philadelphia Museum of Art, for which the Art Institute owns a glowing oil sketch. The finished work has three receding visual planes. On the closest one, the clothes of the woman model are thrown on one chair, and a chaperone sits on another. The clothing the chaperone wears (and the model does not), along with the finished woodwork of the two chairs, stands in bold contrast with the naked model and the rough wood stump she poses on. The model emerges out of the dishevelment of civilized clothes and furniture as if stepping back into an earlier cultural stage, of unadorned nature.

Only on the third, most distant, plane do we see the sculptor dimly at work, surrounded by his other artifacts (of which Eakins modeled clay replicas to get the sculptor's sense of form into his own figures).

Thomas Eakins, *William Rush Carving His Allegorical Figure of the Schuylkill,* 1877. Oil on canvas; 20⅛ × 26½ in. Philadelphia Museum of Art, gift of Mrs. Thomas Eakins and Miss Mary Adeline Williams.

The fountain statue, which all Philadelphians were familiar with from a later bronze copy, was elongated. A tern was perched on the nymph's shoulder, to extend the figure's lines up to the point where water sprang from the tern's mouth and clothed the white statue in a shifting liquid veil. By contrast, the painter's model is chunky, made deliberately awkward in different studies. She is real, palpable, like the women Eakins painted in his portraits—though the model stands with her face away from us. Rush shows her being transmuted by the obscure activity of a master craftsman-idealist. The real action takes place in shadow. All the background, obscurely crammed with

112

Rush's artifacts, is a cave of the imagination where the real becomes more real.

One could almost read the painting as a satire on classicism, since the naked realism of the model is more instantly stunning than the wood artifacts only partly discernible around the workshop. But Eakins honored the craftsman in Rush. The ships' scrolls, seen on the same plane as the model's pedestal, echo the roundness of her hips. Rush was creating, not just copying. In the third (1908) painting, now at the Honolulu Academy of Arts, Rush helps the model off her stump, in a clear reference to the Galatea myth (of which Eakins's teacher, Jean Léon Gérôme, had painted a famous version). Rush has brought the young woman to a higher form of life, a fact emphasized by all the *non*-statuesque aspects of the awkward girl seen in full light, having trouble maneuvering the short steps down from the perch.

The Art Institute sketch (1877), with its overall brown color of the woodworker's studio, contains the allegorical statue of the Philadelphia Waterworks barely visible on the left. Two triangular patches of light below that sculpture serve, as the discarded clothes do in the finished picture, to give a blurry light contrasted with the sharply lit curve of the model's body. Here the model is carved in light out of the wooden colors all around her. The model's upper body is more delicate than in other sketches (or in the first painting). The hips have the roundness of the ship's scroll in other versions. The solidly tactile form has a sculptor's shaping sense, yet it is also evanescent, disappearing, on the right, into the formless dark of the studio. The body is being sculpted before our eye—and behind the artist's eyes. We see creation in mid-act.

In the sketch, as in the first picture, the light is a narrow shaft piercing the darkness. Though Eakins made precise sketches of a room said to resemble Rush's studio, the darkness of the studio in the finished painting is entirely unrealistic. The single shaft is at odds with the equable lighting a sculptor would want on his model and the wood he was working. Despite the trappings of realism, Eakins is painting a highly symbolic picture. The studio is the brain of Rush, and his art is the light that shapes the woman out of this womb of darkness.

SUMMER STORM

As Mondrian knew,
Art is the image of an image of an image,
More vacant, more transparent
With each repeat and slough:
                              one skin, two skins, it comes clear,
An old idea not that old.

Two rectangles, red and gray, from 1935,
Distant thunder like distant thunder—
Howitzer shells, large
                    drop-offs into drumbeat and roll.
And there's that maple again,
Head like an African Ice Age queen, full-leafed and lipped.

Behind her, like clear weather,
Mondrian's window gives out
                          onto ontology,
A dab of red, a dab of gray, white interstices.
You can't see the same thing twice,
As Mondrian knew.

CLAES OLDENBURG'S *CLOTHESPIN* (1975)

Claes Oldenburg's *Clothespin* stands in the Art Institute's palatial halls like a Cyclopean, ten-foot-tall security guard, his gracefully tapered legs braced apart, his spring ready to snap. But the resemblance is incidental, we feel; Oldenburg is too much the engineer and architectural draughtsman to be after anything less than the *Ding an sich,* the thing in itself. His plaster hamburgers, his canvas telephones, his giant typewriter erasers and baseball bats and electrical switches and plugs all have an elemental solemnity that disdains anthropomorphism and beckons us into the mute, inhuman world of artifacts. Oldenburg's sculptures look made, and concern made things.

Somewhat as Renaissance draughtsman like Michelangelo and Dürer "blew up" natural details such as flowers, rabbits, and human musculature under the microscope of their close attention, after the long inattention of the Middle Ages, so the Pop artists, after the mystic self-absorption of the Abstract Expressionists, turned to the circumambient reality of nature, and enlarged it with artistic focus. Their nature, however, was of human manufacture: Jasper Johns dignified flags and beer cans; Andy Warhol transferred to canvas the trash imagery of tabloids and advertising; Roy Lichtenstein seized upon the Benday dots, primary colors, and emphatic outlines of comic strips. There was a joy of reclamation in Pop art, a relieved embrace of the tangible world after the monkish austerities and tragic mood of action painting. Nothing was too lowly to notice—bottle caps, dollar bills, junk food, crushed cars—and to elevate into the museum of the cherishable. Robert Rauschenberg, with such infamous *trouvés* as the stuffed angora goat girdled by an old tire, showed the way; his masters in the Zen contemplation of the conundrum of art were Marcel Duchamp and John Cage. Pop art had, in Dada, an intellectual pedigree. But a number of the Pop artists were doing what came naturally—Warhol had been a commercial artist, James

Rosenquist a billboard painter—and the movement had an unforced connection with American folk art, as it had moved from handmade nineteenth-century artifacts to twentieth-century articles of mass manufacture. Among its several messages *Clothespin* is telling us that this humble utilitarian device is elegant and beautiful.

Irony is a way of having one's cake while appearing to eat it. An effect of Oldenburg's raising the clothespin to monumentality is to mock the concept of monumentality, which has thrust upon Mankind's weary vision so many bloated colossi, emperors' effigies, mounted bronze heroes, gesturing Lenins, gilded Buddhas, and similar ponderous advertisements of creed and hegemony. The monumental asserts establishment values, against not only contemporary dissent but against the erosion of time, unmindful that all monuments become, eventually, the enigmatic pillars of Ozymandias. Eternalization, when applied to an implement for pinching damp clothes to a line, becomes comic, as is this heroic solitude of an item useful only in numbers and generally clustered in a box or basket. The Art Institute's context of fine Doric gallery underlines the satire.

Yet is satire the only point? A true monumentality is achieved. Our childhood apprehensions of reality are revived in the disproportionate glorification of the overlookable; a child overlooks nothing near him, and the contours and mechanism of a clothespin, say, impress him with a huge, though unspeakable, significance. The mute significance of things gives the visual arts their inexhaustible impetus; the visible world, so abundant and heedless around us, is processed, by the painter's or sculptor's hand, and becomes understood. This act of understanding is the light that representation gives off, and that draws millions to rotate through museums, delighting in recognitions. We recognize the clothespin, even though it has been idealized in CorTen and stainless steel, enlarged in size, and placed

upside-down from the way we usually see it on the clothesline. The recognition is fringed and flavored by what art history we possess—by whatever analogies to the Eiffel Tower or Brancusi's *Kiss* arise—but there is no escaping the *Ding an sich*. As with

Oldenburg's forty-five-foot *Clothespin* near City Hall in Philadelphia, or the hundred-foot *Baseball Bat* that adorns Chicago, a humble bit of our lives is given large public dignity, in a kind of democratic revolution.

117

THE FATHER'S HOUSE

Here, as in childhood, Brother, no one knows us.
And someone has died, and someone is not yet

born, while our father walks through his church at night
and sets all the clocks for spring. His sleeplessness

weighs heavy on my forehead, his death almost
nothing. In the only letter he wrote to us

he says, *No one can tell how long it takes a seed*
to declare what death and lightning told it

while it slept. But stand at a window long enough,
late enough, and you may some night hear

a secret you'll tomorrow, parallel to the morning,
tell on a wide, white bed, to a woman

like a sown ledge of wheat. Or you may never
tell it, who lean across the night and miles of the sea,

to arrive at a seed, in whose lamplit house
resides a thorn, or a wee man, carving

a name on a stone, at a fluctuating table of water,
the name of the one who has died, the name of the one

not born unknown. Someone has died. Someone
is not yet born. And during this black interval,

I sweep all three floors of our father's house,
and I don't count the broom strokes; I row

up and down for nothing but love: his for me, and my own
for the threshold, as well as for the woman's name

I hear while I sweep, as though she swept
beside me, a woman who, if she owns a face at all,

it is its own changing; and if I know her name
I know to say it so softly she need not

stop her work to hear me. But when she lies down
at night, in the room of our arrival, she'll know

I called her, though she won't answer, who is on her way
to sleep, until morning, which even now,

is overwhelming, the woman combing her hair
opposite the direction of my departure.

And only now and then do I lean at a jamb
to see if I can see what I thought I heard.

I heard her ask, *My love, why can't you sleep?*
and answer, *Someone has died, and someone*

is not yet born. Meanwhile, I hear the voices
of women telling a story in the round,

so I sit down on a rain-eaten stoop, by the saltgrasses,
and go on folding the laundry I was folding,

the everyday clothes of our everyday life, the death
clothes wearing us clean to the bone, to the very

ilium crest, where my right hand, this hand, half
crab, part bird, has often come to rest on her,

whose name I know. And because I sat down,
I hear their folding sound, and know

the tide is rising early, and I can't hope
to trap their story told in the round. But the woman

whose name I know says, *Sleep*, so I lie down
on the clothes, the folded and unfolded, the life

and the death. Ages go by. When I wake, the story
has changed the firmament into domain, domain

into a house. And the sun speaks the day,
unnaming, showing the story, dissipating the boundaries

of the telling, to include the one who has died
and the one not yet born. Someone has died

and someone is not yet born. How still
this morning grows about the voice of one

child reading to another, how much a house
is house at all due to one room where an elder

child reads to his brother, and that younger
knows by heart the brother-voice. How darker

other rooms stand, how slow morning comes, collected
in a name, told at one sill and listened for

at the threshold of dew. What book is this we read
together, Brother, and at which window

of our father's house? In which upper room?
We read it twice: Once in two voices, to each

other; once in unison, to children,
animals, and the sun, our star, that vast office

of love, the one we sit in once, and read
together twice, the third time bosomed in

the future. So birds may lend their church, sown
in air, realized in the body uttering

windows, growing rafters, couching seeds.

JOSEPH CORNELL'S *HÔTEL DU NORD*

The windows of Hôtel du Nord have a view of the snows of Labrador which are famous for their yellow sunflowers. The white paint in our room is peeling; the beds and chairs have gone to China to be missionaries; the desk clerk is as deaf as a shoe brush. The hermit architect was thinking about his invalid brother's toy box and a flytrap in his mother's kitchen. When somebody knocked, we ran to open. There was never anyone. The quiet that reigns in the hotel is that of an Egyptian pyramid in a hundred-year-old postcard with an address in Oklahoma on the other side.

The sky is blue and so is the ceiling. Glued to the wall, there's a cut-out of a Renaissance child pointing to a picture of a camel that could have come out of a long discontinued breakfast cereal. Above him, hung from a silver rod by a metal hook, there's a stamp with a picture of another smaller Renaissance child. This one appears to be saying his bedtime prayer. Their father, the Prince, has gone off to stand on the parapet with his beard on fire.

Time hesitates between dream and reality with the key in the door; the tongue can't find a word in the whole wide world. Solitude has a spidery stepladder which it is going to climb and peek at the boar with tusks hidden behind the white column. If night ever falls, the two children will light matches and eat dragon stew.

THE EARLIEST ANGELS

The earliest angels were swarthy, stooped,
hairy, with a flat forehead
and crested skulls,
arms down to the knees. In place of wings
just two parachutes of skin,
a kind of black flying squirrel
in the volcanic winds.

Totally trustworthy.
They performed astounding miracles.
Transubstantiations. Metamorphoses
of mud into mud fish.
A rocking horse,
inflated to heavenly size,
atomic fusion at room temperature,
holding up the mirror,
stirrings of consciousness,
creating the majesty of death.

They worked hard.
They tinkered with graves.
They swam in murky waters.
They huddled in oviducts.
They hid behind the door.

They waited.
                    They waited in vain.

(Translated by David Young and Dennis O'Driscoll)

JORIE GRAHAM
On Anselm Kiefer, *The Order of the Angels*, 1983/84

THE FIELD

1.

Before, there is this field.

And after, too, we are in the same field.

Before, it is dark and we can't yet see it: we stand
in it: we feel our standing like a spindle, turning, twisting
                                        in its
strange homesickness, strands of the looking-out which leak, flaxen,
                                                    from us
blinking in the dark, so quiet, gazelle of furling
                        imaginings
—oh overgrown eye!—awaiting, in the gossamer of looking
: some supple yet resistant clutter
: suddenly multi-faceted, edges emerging
: one big one at the top, horizontal, like an ending
: crepe-like (incomparably soft) the sides: like wings
: yes, in the field of the periphery (head still—
                        eyes forward—)
: the sides (just beyond actual seeing), the sides fetched-up with
                        coarse spectrums, outskirts of
the betrothal: almost a sensation of regret,
as where a voice, still calling-out, does enter finally the
                                        inaudible
: and you know they can't see you anymore so why are you
: still standing here: why: why?: unless of course
you turn your head: there now: efficient: (why the
                        sound in the
                        inaudible
like a cough? or a spade stabbing soil? a wedge of snow
                        falling of itself

126

onto the snow): there now, you can begin again: again:
the eyes starting the story afresh, bits connected,
                                        the whole
                                        philosophical
vertigo molting your glances—(more and more of them)—off
                                                    its spoked
long-distanced, stringy, muddy (with what?)
debris—a delirium—furrowed—mudtroughs, mudripplings
                                        everywhere—
equality the terror—equality of *all seen*
                        things—gaze like
                        a fabric
dropped hissing through the open and then down, like a stillness,
onto:

                                2.

So, now, we are in this field and it is the start
of day. It is deep with what appears to be
mud. Actually what has opened the soil and made it
                                        exuberant,
made it snarl with suctions and tiny, momentary, frontiers,
is blood. Enough blood to cough up
                        the underloam
—and footsteps, and the weight of many bodies, heavy
                                        equipment
(grammatical swirlings of
tire-tread, tank-tread—
if there were horses one cannot tell) . . . It looks,
                                of course,

now that the bodies have been taken away
each to its own luminous personality—name and number—
and now that what can be salvaged of the munitions
has been, each to its own purpose, washed-clean, re-
                                built—

it looks (if only the sun would come out) like any field
in which the work of humans has distended itself—site, set,
                                                field of

vision—there is a bit of cyclone fence (barbed wire?)

which the mud has, upswirling, taken into itself,
you can see where its ribs are each now erased
                              in newly-ribbed
mud, you can see where the mud is joying a pattern,
you can see where six large boulders are holding down

the bureaucracy of mud, where its powers must, swirling,
                                    reassign themselves,
slipping upwards in yieldings that become aggressions, up-
                                    thrusting
enhancements, furrows and furrows of matter being made to
                                    re-place
itself. A new place. Yet remember the wetness in it, how
                              it will shape
                                    the dirt into waves.
Remember the liquidity spiraling up in this heavy
                              mediation
and then, as the sun returns (when the sun will return)
how it will harden into the shape of how free
                              it had been.
Remember though what imbues it.
Not red—the soil has taken the color. Not simply viscous—

this soil is full of clay to begin with. . . . And remember, too,

how all the bodies, all the sources

of the wavelike frothings of this quickened soil

have been lifted one by one and claimed and cleaned.

2a.

So much blood the whole field was opened by it.

And still is open after all this time.

Remember that the bodies (and machines) were recovered.

Place them on the field again (27,000), spread out their limbs, rip their
garments, a sleeve, a shoulder—let them catch light—
(so you can see)—then lift them away, one by one, up out of the mud—

then come back with the others to get the machines—clear them out—there,

you have it now: the field.

3.

Today I am gazing at it in this book. I look up suddenly, now,
a man runs across my yard screaming *Roger, Roger*—hoarse, large with
                                        rage—his black
                                        dog leaping
wildly   ahead   of   him,   staying   so.

4.

In the air of this room, in what slavers under
                        this layer
                        of listening,
I can hear, through the speakers, fingers on
                        the piano keys—
then a pushing (a sound beneath) a susurration of
                        busy desire
                        (or fear?)

—not a clicking (as of fingernails)—but the pressure
                                    in the making
                                    of the thing
made—the making of the note distinct from
                                    the intended
note—distinct also from the heard

note—distinct from the imagined note. Just where
                                    it pushes free,

where the hands go into the machine to want to
                                    find and then
                                    to find.

5.

Outside, smoke rises between the houses. I look carefully. Nobody
                                    there.

CHARLES BAXTER
On John La Farge, *Snow Field, Morning, Roxbury,* 1864

DESCENT OF ANGELS

> "Americanly innocent."
> —Henry James, speaking of John La Farge

Almost every afternoon during the winter of 1870, around two o'clock, the young mother bundled up her baby in his snowsuit and went out to sit on the bench in the backyard. She always cleared the bench of the new snow with her gloved free hand; then she sat down with the baby perched on her knee. There, she gazed at the snow field to the west. The woods started three quarters of a mile back in the distance, and after tilting her head to check on the boy, Thomas, she would turn back to face the trees, the horizon tilted now, higher on the right side than on the left, as if everything in her field of vision had an inclination to slide toward the south.

She and her husband had been married for only nineteen months, and she was still so in love with him that she measured the shadows on the ground to gauge the amount of time until twilight and his return. She considered herself a rather plain woman, though with certain good features, including a pleasant sense of humor and pretty hands. Her physical urgency for her husband had caught her a bit by surprise. Even with the constant chores and the baby's requirements, she would wait for her husband to return and for the moment when her flesh would press against his. He was a country doctor beginning practice, tall and sandy-haired, with a light mustache, who was pleased and surprised by his wife's ardor and who on most nights was eager to return it.

She liked to gaze at the four small evergreens just in front of her and to think of them as a family, surviving somehow in the midst of nothing special, just a blank full gaze of whiteness. The largest tree, the one on the left, would be her husband, Samuel. Sometimes, however, she thought of herself as that tree, as Samuel, as the strongest one, the one who stayed and stayed and stayed. The tree next to it was herself, usually, and the two seedlings next to that were their two children, the one

they had already had, Thomas, and the second one they would have some day, Louisa.

Thomas stirred in her lap and reached up a mittened hand to her, as if he knew that hidden in her coat and sweater and shirt and undergarments there was still a breast, and he could nurse there. He was five months old and was a strong observant child, full of lusty good cheer and cries and curiosity. He occupied her days, and, even as she scrubbed the floor, she had developed the habit of speaking to him as she would to a companion, telling him all her secrets, even a few intimate ones that she guessed a child should not hear.

Gazing at the woods, she liked to imagine someone emerging from the trees and crossing the snow field to rescue her. But no: she didn't need rescuing: her husband would return as he always did, and she was here, and she was fine, more or less.

Because of a childhood accident, she was radically color-blind. When people spoke of a thing's being "blue," or "red," she had only the dimmest idea of what they meant. To her, the scenes of the world came to her with all the hues silent and muted. This sky, for example, was gray, and the clouds above it were gray, and the snow field, of course, was white discolored by brown. She could still sometimes see brown. She knew her son's eyes were blue because people had told her so. It was her sole heartbreak not to see the color of his eyes.

From behind her, behind the house, she heard a bird, a crow, followed, very distantly, by the barking of a dog.

"There they are," she said. "The animals. Do you hear them?" She kissed Thomas on the forehead to help him hear.

But he was not listening. He was watching the snow field and the sky above it. His gaze was transfixed. He sat utterly still. In this attitude, his body was rigid with attentiveness,

132

with the claim of some distinct spiritous phantom. His eyes were open so wide they seemed baby-shocked. She turned to see what he saw.

Whatever it was, it was descending. From the ash trails of the lethargic clouds, countless human forms, cloaked only in radiance, sung their way silently through the air toward her and then stopped as if in midair, to the left of the family of evergreens, hovering there in beatitude.

Male and female, and inexplicitly beautiful in their forms, passing back and forth in mystery their joy and sanctity, they caused in her a shock of unpleasant peacefulness. She had not known her loneliness could give rise to this. Robed in light, and naked beneath the light, they were standing together, not terrible but not earthly, their feelings larger than they were. She was washed in their light. She clutched her son, who had seen them first. They were not as they had been described in Scrip-

ture. Against the blankness of the snow field they asserted their presence to her. Then they returned to their realm, and she was left with her baby, and the snow field with its woods and gray light, and the perpetuity of the cold hillside.

They had been here, she judged, for ten seconds.

How many of us have seen a thing about which we could never speak? An event so large and private and wondrous, so beyond description, and so secret, that even to begin to explain it would cast the world's doubt on us, and so spoil it? She was a simple American woman, a young mother who had seen what could not be sanely described. She gathered up her son to her shoulder and carried him inside. She was weeping with the joy and secrecy of it. Alone with her child in her house, she fell to her knees and removed his snowsuit; she did not know how to pray, so she undressed him and herself and put him to her breast.

When her husband came home that evening, she did not speak of it. Through the dinner and his talk, she was hushed. She cast over herself an invisible veil. She could not remove from her mind the image of the snow field, the family of evergreens, the tilted horizon, and the spirits in the emptiness. That night, with the baby sleeping, she asked her husband to undress with the lights still burning. He was puzzled but did as she asked; then she disrobed herself. She saw how moved he was by her beauty. She saw his lineaments of action and desire, and she felt herself begin to weep again, wondering how long her husband and she herself would survive her vision. She pressed her color-blind eyes against his chest and wiped her tears on his skin.

ELLEN BRYANT VOIGT
On Georgia O'Keeffe, *Black Cross, New Mexico, 1929*

WORMWOOD: THE PENITENTS

I always thought she ought to have an angel.
There's one I saw a picture of, smooth white,
the wings like bolts of silk, breasts like a girl's—
like hers—eyebrows, all of it. Ten years
I put away a little every year,
but her family was shamed by the bare grave,
and wasn't I to blame for everything,
so now she has a cross. Crude, rigid, nothing
human in it, flat dead tree on the hill,
it's what you see for miles, it's all I see.
Symbol of hope, the priest said, clearing his throat,
and the rain came down and washed the plastic flowers.
I guess he thinks that dusk is just like dawn.
I guess he had forgot about the nails.

CHECKLIST

Ivan Albright
(American, 1897–1983)
Into the World There Came a Soul Called Ida, 1929–30
Oil on canvas; 56¼ × 47 in. (142.9 × 119.2 cm)
Gift of Ivan Albright, 1977.34

Self-Portrait (no. 10), 1982
Colored pastel on hardboard; 13 × 10 in. (33 × 25.4 cm)
Gift of Mrs. Ivan Albright, 1985.425

Self-Portrait (no. 19), 1983
Colored pencils on hardboard; 12 × 10 in. (30.5 × 25.4 cm)
Gift of Mrs. Ivan Albright, 1985.434

Self-Portrait (no. 21), 1983
Pencil and colored pencil on primed hardboard; 13 × 10 in. (33 × 25.4 cm)
Gift of Mrs. Ivan Albright, 1985.436

Diane Arbus
(American, 1923–1971)
Two Ladies at the Automat (New York City), 1966
Silver-gelatin print; 14¾ × 14¾ in. (374 × 374 mm)
Gift of Theodore Collyer, 1981.557

Francis Bacon
(English, b. Ireland, 1910–1992)
Figure with Meat, 1954
Oil on canvas; 51⅛ × 48 in. (129.9 × 121.9 cm)
Harriet A. Fox Fund, 1956.1201

Peter Blume
(American, b. Russia, 1906–1992)
The Rock, 1943
Oil on canvas; 57⅝ × 74⅜ in. (146.4 × 188.9 cm)
Gift of Edgar Kaufmann, Jr., 1956.338

Eugène Boudin
(French, 1824–1898)
Approaching Storm, 1864
Oil on panel; 14⅜ × 22¾ in. (36.6 × 57.9 cm)
Mr. and Mrs. Lewis Larned Coburn Memorial Collection, 1938.1276

Constantin Brancusi
(French, b. Romania, 1876–1957)
Golden Bird, 1919/20, pedestal c. 1922
Bronze, stone, and wood; h. 37¾ in. (95.9 cm)
Partial gift of the Arts Club of Chicago; restricted gift of various donors; through prior bequest of Arthur Rubloff; through prior restricted gift of William Hartmann; through prior gifts of Mr. and Mrs. Carter H. Harrison, Mr. and Mrs. Arnold H. Maremont through the Kate Maremont Foundation, Woodruff J. Parker, Mrs. Clive Runnells, Mr. and Mrs. Martin A. Ryerson, and various donors, 1990.88

Jules Breton
(French, 1827–1906)
The Song of the Lark, 1884
Oil on canvas; 43½ × 33¾ in. (110.6 × 85.8 cm)
Henry Field Memorial Collection, 1894.1033

Mary Cassatt
(American, 1844–1926)
Woman Bathing, 1891
Drypoint and aquatint printed in color from three plates, on white laid paper; 14¼ × 10½ in. (363 × 265 mm)
Mr. and Mrs. Martin A. Ryerson Collection, 1932.1281

Giorgio de Chirico
(Italian, 1888–1978)
The Philosopher's Conquest, 1914
Oil on canvas; 49¼ × 39 in. (125.1 × 99.1 cm)
Joseph Winterbotham Collection, 1939.405

Joseph Cornell
(American, 1903–1972)
Untitled (Hôtel du Nord), c. 1950
Painted, glazed wooden box with paper backing for a kinetic assemblage of wood, paint, paper, graphite, photographs, metal rod, and postage stamp; 18½ × 12⅜ × 4½ in. (47.1 × 31.4 × 11.4 cm)
Lindy and Edwin Bergman Collection, 1982.1855

Edgar Degas
(French, 1834–1917)
Portrait after a Costume Ball (Portrait of Mme Dietz-Monnin), 1877/79
Distemper, with metallic paint and pastel, on canvas; 33⅝ × 29½ in.
(88.5 × 75 cm)
Joseph Winterbotham Collection, 1954.325

Ballet at the Paris Opéra, 1877
Pastel over monotype on cream laid paper; 14⅛ × 28¼ in. (359 × 719 mm)
Gift of Mary and Leigh Block, 1981.12

The Millinery Shop, 1879/84
Oil on canvas; 39⅜ × 43⅝ in. (100 × 110.7 cm)
Mr. and Mrs. Lewis Larned Coburn Memorial Collection, 1933.428

Robert Delaunay
(French, 1885–1941)
Champs de Mars: The Red Tower, begun in 1911, revised sometime before 1923
Oil on canvas; 64 × 51½ in. (163 × 131 cm)
Joseph Winterbotham Collection, 1959.1

Thomas Eakins
(American, 1844–1916)
Study for *William Rush Carving His Allegorical Figure of the Schuylkill River,* 1877
Oil on canvas; 14⅛ × 11¼ in. (35.9 × 28.6 cm)
Bequest of Dr. John J. Ireland, 1968.91

Henri Fantin-Latour
(French, 1836–1904)
Still Life: Corner of a Table, 1873
Oil on canvas; 37⅞ × 49⅛ in. (96.4 × 125 cm)
Ada Turnbull Hertle Fund, 1951.226

Lyonel Feininger (Charles Leonell Feininger)
(American, 1871–1956)
Carnival in Arcueil, 1911
Oil on canvas; 41¼ × 37¾ in. (105 × 96 cm)
Joseph Winterbotham Collection, 1990.119

Paul Gauguin
(French, 1848–1903)
Pape Moe (Mysterious Water), c. 1893
Watercolor on ivory wove paper; 13⅞ × 10 in. (355 × 255 mm)
Gift of Mrs. Emily Crane Chadbourne, 1922.4797

Leon Golub
(American, b. 1922)
Interrogation II, 1981
Acrylic on canvas; 120 × 168 in. (304.8 × 427.7 cm)
Gift of the Society for Contemporary Art, 1983.264

Francisco Goya y Lucientes
(Spanish, 1746–1828)
Estragos de la Guerra (Ravages of War), 1863
Plate 30 from *The Disasters of War*
Etching, drypoint, burin, and burnisher on paper; 5⅝ × 6⅝ in.
(141 × 167 mm)
Gift of J. C. Cebrian, 1920.1335

Qué hai que hacer mas? (What more can be done?), 1863
Plate 33 from *The Disasters of War*
Etching, lavis, drypoint, burin, and burnisher on paper; 9½ × 13¼ in.
(240 × 339 mm)
Gift of J. C. Cebrian, 1920.1338

No hay quien los socorra (There is no one to help them), 1863
Plate 60 from *The Disasters of War*
Etching, burnished aquatint, burin, and burnisher on paper; 5⅞ × 8⅛ in.
(150 × 205 mm)
Gift of J. C. Cebrian, 1920.1365

Sí son de otro linage (Perhaps they are of another breed), 1863
Plate 61 from *The Disasters of War*
Etching, lavis, drypoint, burin, and burnisher on paper; 6⅛ × 8⅛ in.
(155 × 205 mm)
Gift of J. C. Cebrian, 1920.1366

Philip Guston
(American, b. Canada, 1913–1980)
Green Sea, 1976
Oil on canvas; 70 × 116½ in. (177.8 × 295.9 cm)
Restricted gift of Mrs. Frederic G. Pick; Grant J. Pick, Charles H. and
Mary F. S. Worcester, Twentieth-Century Discretionary Fund; anony-
mous gift, 1985.1118

Edward Hopper
(American, 1882–1967)
Nighthawks, 1942
Oil on canvas; 33⅛ × 60 in. (84.1 × 152.4 cm)
Friends of American Art Collection, 1942.51

Jasper Johns
(American, b. 1930)
Corpse and Mirror II, 1974–75
Oil on canvas; 57½ × 75 in. (146.1 × 190.5 cm)
Lent by the artist, 7.1976

Anselm Kiefer
(German, b. 1945)
The Order of the Angels, 1983/84
Oil, acrylic, emulsion, shellac, and straw on canvas with cardboard and lead;
129⅞ × 218½ in. (330 × 555 cm)
Restricted gift of the Nathan Manilow Foundation; Lewis and Susan Manilow,
Samuel A. Marx Funds, 1985.243

Paul Klee
(German, b. Switzerland, 1879–1940)
Strange Glance, 1930
Oil on canvas; 25¾ × 15 in. (65.4 × 38.1 cm)
Gift of Claire Zeisler, 1991.320

John La Farge
(American, 1835–1910)
Snow Field, Morning, Roxbury, 1864
Oil on beveled mahogany panel; 12 × 9⅞ in. (30.5 × 25.1 cm)
Mrs. Frank L. Sulzberger Fund in memory of Mr. Frank L. Sulzberger, 1981.287

Li-Lin Lee
(American, b. Indonesia, 1955)
Corban Ephphatha I, 1991/92
Oil and alkyd on burlap, mounted on canvas; 70 × 54 in. (178 × 137 cm)
Twentieth-Century Discretionary Fund, 1992.288

Henri Matisse
(French, 1869–1954)
Woman Before an Aquarium, 1921
Oil on canvas; 31¾ × 39⅜ in. (80.7 × 100 cm)
Helen Birch Bartlett Memorial Collection, 1926.200

Joan Miró
(Spanish, 1893–1983)
Portrait of a Woman (Juanita Obrador), 1918
Oil on canvas; 27⅜ × 24⅜ in. (69.5 × 62 cm)
Joseph Winterbotham Collection, 1957.78

Piet Mondrian
(Dutch, 1872–1944)
Composition—Gray Red, 1935
Oil on canvas; 21⅝ × 22⅜ in. (55 × 57 cm)
Gift of Mrs. Gilbert W. Chapman, 1949.518

Claude Monet
(French, 1840–1926)
Sandvika, Norway, 1895
Oil on canvas; 28⅞ × 36⅜ in. (73.4 × 92.5 cm)
Gift of Bruce Borland, 1961.790

Water Lilies, 1906
Oil on canvas; 34½ × 36½ in. (87.6 × 92.7 cm)
Mr. and Mrs. Martin A. Ryerson Collection, 1933.1157

William Sidney Mount
(American, 1807–1868)
Walking the Line, 1835
Oil on canvas; 22⅝ × 27½ in. (57.5 × 69.7 cm)
Goodman Fund, 1939.392

Georgia O'Keeffe
(American, 1887–1986)
Black Cross, New Mexico, 1929
Oil on canvas; 39 × 30⅛ in. (99.2 × 76.3 cm)
Art Institute Purchase Fund, 1943.95

Claes Oldenburg
(American, b. Sweden, 1929)
Clothespin, 1975
CorTen and stainless steel; h. 120 in. (304.8 cm)
Gift of the Auxiliary Board; Mr. and Mrs. Frank G. Logan Prize Fund, 1976.96

Pablo Picasso
(Spanish, 1881–1973)
The Old Guitarist, 1903
Oil on panel; 48⅛ × 32½ in. (122.9 × 82.6 cm)
Helen Birch Bartlett Memorial Collection, 1926.253

Auguste Rodin
(French, 1840–1917)
The Walking Man, c. 1900
Bronze; h. 33⅛ in. (84.1 cm)
Bequest of A. James Speyer, 1987.217

Georges Seurat
(French, 1859–1891)
A Sunday on La Grande Jatte—1884, 1884–86
Oil on canvas; 81⅝ × 121¼ in. (207.6 × 308 cm)
Helen Birch Bartlett Memorial Collection, 1926.224

Charles Sheeler
(American, 1882–1967)
The Artist Looks at Nature, 1943
Oil on canvas; 21 × 18 in. (53.3 × 45.7 cm)
Gift of the Society for Contemporary American Art, 1944.32

Chaim Soutine
(Lithuanian, 1893–1943)
Dead Fowl, 1926
Oil on canvas; 38⅜ × 24⅞ in. (97.5 × 63.2 cm)
Joseph Winterbotham Collection, 1937.167

Wayne Thiebaud
(American, b. 1920)
Steep Street, 1989
Drypoint and spitbite aquatint on paper; 21¾ × 29¾ in. (555 × 756 mm)
Restricted gift of Phil Shorr and the Wayne Thiebaud Family to honor the memory of Ruth L. Shorr, 1990.460

Henri de Toulouse-Lautrec
(French, 1864–1901)
At the Moulin Rouge, 1892/95
Oil on canvas; 48½ × 55½ in. (123 × 141 cm)
Helen Birch Bartlett Memorial Collection, 1928.610

Grant Wood
(American, 1891–1942)
American Gothic, 1930
Oil on beaver board; 29¼ × 24⅝ in. (74.3 × 62.4 cm)
Friends of American Art Collection, 1930.934

BIOGRAPHICAL INDEX OF ARTISTS AND WRITERS

ARTISTS

Ivan Albright (1897–1983) was born in a suburb of Chicago and spent most of his life in and around the city. Deeply influenced by his experience as a medical illustrator during World War I, he painted highly detailed portrayals of aging and decay in a style that has been called Magic Realism.

Diane Arbus (1923–1971) was an American photographer known for the directness and uncomfortable intimacy of her photographs of the eccentric and the extreme, including dwarfs, transvestites, giants, and nudists.

Francis Bacon (1909–1992) was a self-taught painter who became one of the best-known British artists of his era. His bleak and often nihilistic depictions of tortured and deformed figures frequently relate to historical and literary sources.

Peter Blume (1906–1992) was born in Russia, but spent most of his life in the United States, where he was influenced by European and American movements such as Surrealism and Precisionism. Images of disintegration and rebirth often occur in his work, which is based on the juxtaposition of disjunctive and unrelated objects and figures, rendered in a highly realistic style reminiscent of northern European Renaissance painting.

Eugène Boudin (1824–1898), a French painter, was a teacher of Impressionist painter Claude Monet. He is best known for his delicate beach scenes and seascapes, which demonstrate his interest in depicting the play of light in nature, a subject later explored by the Impressionists.

Constantin Brancusi (1876–1957) was born in Romania and settled in Paris in 1904. A preeminent sculptor, he created variations on several themes, often in a range of media, making each version a meditation on some primary form.

Jules Breton (1827–1906), a French painter with strong academic training, became known for his naturalistic, if at times idealized, depictions of rustic life.

Mary Cassatt (1844–1926) was an accomplished American painter and printmaker who settled in Paris. In 1877 she was invited by Edgar Degas to become the first American to exhibit with the French Impressionists. Cassatt often depicted domestic life, especially that of upper-class women and their children.

Giorgio de Chirico (1888–1978) created precise depictions of silent, deserted urban and imaginary spaces illuminated in a cold, white light. His mysterious works profoundly affected the Surrealists' attempts to portray dreams and images of the subconscious.

Joseph Cornell (1903–1972), a reclusive American artist, was a pioneer in the art of assemblage. His celebrated boxes house poetic combinations of found objects and materials that relate both to his childhood and adult interests.

Edgar Degas (1834–1917), a French Impressionist painter, draftsman, printmaker, and sculptor, was one of the nineteenth century's most innovative artists. He often combined traditional techniques in unorthodox ways and is best known for his subtle portraits and scenes of the ballet and theater.

Robert Delaunay (1885–1941) was a French painter who fashioned a visual language he called Simultaneity, largely adapted from Cubism and influenced by nineteenth-century color theory, to depict the dynamism of modern life and the abstract qualities of color.

Thomas Eakins (1844–1916) was one of the greatest American artists of his time. A native of Philadelphia, to which he returned after training in Europe, he was a teacher, photographer, and sculptor, as well as a painter. An uncompromising realism characterizes all of his work, which includes portraiture, scientific and genre subjects, and outdoor scenes.

Henri Fantin-Latour (1836–1904) was a French painter and lithographer. His still lifes of luxurious flowers set against neutral backgrounds are distinguished by their careful compositions and precise detail.

Lyonel Feininger (1871–1956) was born in New York City to German parents, and spent much of his career in Germany. His early work reflects his experience as a cartoonist, and his frequent use of angular lines and broken planes links him to the Cubist and Futurist movements.

Paul Gauguin (1848–1903), a French painter with South American Indian ancestry, left a profitable career in business to pursue art. His sojourns in Brittany, the south of France, the Caribbean, and the South Pacific, where he was to spend all but two of the last fifteen years of his life, influenced his interest in primitivism and his highly symbolic imagery.

Leon Golub (born 1922), a native of Chicago who lives in New York City, focuses his work on inhumanity and injustice. His often harrowing paintings are the expression of his belief that art can effect social and political change.

Francisco Goya (1746–1828), a Spaniard, was one of the greatest painters and draftsmen of his time. This highly intelligent artist was interested in the whole range of human experience, including contemporary Spanish events.

Philip Guston (1913–1980) was born in Canada and moved to the United States in 1916. He began his career as a muralist, then became a leading Abstract Expressionist. Around 1970, he developed a direct, richly painted, almost cartoonish figurative style, creating a haunting and influential series of autobiographical images.

Edward Hopper (1882–1967) painted, with clarity and forcefulness, familiar aspects of American life, including city streets, architectural interiors and exteriors, country roads, and the Atlantic coastline. The evocative power of his work lies in his sophisticated use of composition, expressive lighting, and simplified shapes.

Jasper Johns (born 1930), a native of Augusta, Georgia, is one of the pioneers of Pop Art. Best known for his series of targets, flags, and numbers, which he rendered with great precision, Johns continues to "borrow" subject matter from daily life. He lives in New York City.

Anselm Kiefer (born 1945) grew up in post-war Germany. His spectacular, large-scale paintings are laden with expressive power and complex themes relating to nationalism and imperialism, destruction and resurrection, mythology and the occult. His original technique involves loading his supports with such materials as straw, lead, and clay; and blistering the surfaces with heat.

Paul Klee (1879–1940), an inventive and prolific artist, was born in Switzerland and trained in Germany, where he taught at the famed Bauhaus school of design until 1931. Working in a myriad of styles and media, he produced an oeuvre of imagination, mysticism, and supreme technical proficiency, that, along with his legendary teaching skills, made him one of the undisputed masters of twentieth-century art.

John La Farge (1835–1910) became renowned for his domestic and ecclesiastical decorative projects, such as his mural and stained-glass designs for Trinity Church, Boston. He was also recognized for his sensitive and carefully crafted landscapes and floral still lifes, which are among his earlier paintings.

Li-Lin Lee (born 1955) was born in Jakarta, Indonesia, and lives in Chicago. Raised in western Pennsylvania, where his father was a Presbyterian minister, Lee has been influenced by a wide range of religious beliefs to create paintings that express a balance between the spiritual and the physical worlds.

Henri Matisse (1869–1954), along with Pablo Picasso, is considered by many the preeminent artist of his time. A superb colorist who was motivated by the desire to eliminate details and to simplify and purify shape and line, he began his career as a painter, later turning to sculpture, the graphic arts, and collage.

Joan Miró (1893–1944) had a long and prolific career, moving from early Cubist works to the Surrealism and abstraction that are the hallmarks of his mature style. A painter of poetic fantasy and wit, the Spanish painter formulated a personal vocabulary of biomorphic shapes and brilliant color that seems to plumb the subconscious world.

Piet Mondrian (1872–1944) pursued a language of extreme abstraction in order to express the order and unity of nature. By reducing natural forms to their purest linear and color equivalents, he constructed his famous composi-

tions of vertical and horizontal lines in a palette of primary colors, along with black, white, and gray, in a style he termed Neo-Plasticism.

Claude Monet (1840–1926), the most celebrated of the French Impressionists, is perhaps best known for his depictions of outdoor scenes, particularly of his garden at Giverny, and his series of paintings of motifs such as haystacks and the cathedral of Rouen, France, at different times of day.

William Sidney Mount (1807–1868) depicted rural life in the United States, especially New England, often including moral lessons or addressing racial and class issues. The painter used sensitive tonal effects, crisp colors, and carefully balanced compositions.

Georgia O'Keeffe (1887–1986), a leading figure of American modernism, attended The School of The Art Institute of Chicago. One of the avant-garde artists who exhibited at Alfred Stieglitz's gallery 291 in New York, she magnified shapes and simplified details to underscore the beauty of such subjects as flowers, buildings, and desert scenes. She settled permanently in New Mexico in 1949.

Claes Oldenburg (born 1929), born in Sweden, pioneered the "happening" and became a prominent American Pop artist known for his soft sculptures and giant replicas of everyday objects.

Pablo Picasso (1881–1973) had a remarkable artistic career that spanned more than seven decades and influenced nearly every major trend in the first half of the twentieth century. A cofounder of Cubism, the Spanish painter and sculptor was an extraordinarily gifted draftsman and had a great facility for many mediums and techniques.

Auguste Rodin (1840–1917) was widely recognized as the greatest sculptor of his time. He explored the expressive potential of the human body and issues of spatial composition in Romantic works of great skill and power.

Georges Seurat (1859–1891), in his desire to surpass the achievements of Impressionism, developed his own scientific approach to painting. He juxtaposed tiny dots of color to create hues that he believed, through optical blending, had greater luminosity than colors mixed with black or white. This style was eventually called Neo-Impressionism or Pointillism.

Charles Sheeler (1882–1967) was an early American modernist painter and photographer who drew his inspiration from the world of man-made objects. He developed a representational style known as Precisionism, using a hard-edged, controlled technique to depict architectural and industrial subjects, as well as interiors.

Chaim Soutine (1893–1943) was born in Russia and later settled in Paris. An expressionist painter, he used thick brushwork to create turbulent and emotional canvases in which feeling is as important as form.

Wayne Thiebaud (born 1920) is an American Pop artist best known for still lifes of mass-produced cafeteria foodstuffs—cakes, pies, pastries, and so forth—that emphasize the assembly-line character of "fresh-food" products in a consumer society.

Henri de Toulouse-Lautrec (1864–1901), a French painter, draftsman, and lithographer, focused on the activity in the theaters, music halls, and cafes of modern Paris. The daring compositions, dramatic croppings, and flat planes of strident color in his paintings paralleled his radical designs for street posters used as advertisements.

Grant Wood (1891–1942) settled in Iowa, where he was born, after traveling in Europe in the early 1920s. He became increasingly appreciative of the traditions and culture of the Midwest. Influenced as well by Flemish Renaissance art, he intended his work to be a positive statement about the ethics and values of the American heartland.

WRITERS

Charles Baxter (born 1947) is the author of two novels, most recently *Shadow Play,* and three books of stories, including *A Relative Stranger* and *Through the Safety Net.* He lives in Ann Arbor, where he teaches at the University of Michigan.

Saul Bellow (born 1915) is a Canadian-born, American novelist who won the Pulitzer Prize in 1975 for his novel *Humboldt's Gift,* and the Nobel Prize for Literature in 1976. Formerly a professor at the University of Chicago, he currently teaches at Boston University.

Willa Cather (1873–1947) was born in Virginia and attended the University of Nebraska. Her works include one volume of poetry, twelve novels, four collections of short stories, and two of essays. Cather won the Pulitzer Prize in 1923 for *One Of Ours.*

Blaise Cendrars (1887–1961) was a Swiss-born, French poet, filmmaker, and novelist. His use of innovative poetic techniques and imagery drawn from modern life was influenced by Cubism, Dadaism, and Surrealism.

Amy Clampitt (born 1920), a native of Iowa, is the author of five volumes of poetry—most recently, *A Silence Opens*—and a book of essays, *Predecessors, Et Cetera.* Clampitt was awarded a MacArthur Fellowship in 1992. She currently lives in New York City.

Guy Davenport (born 1927), a native of South Carolina, is the author of six collections of short stories, the most recent being *A Table of Green Fields,* published in 1994, the same year as his book *Charles Burchfield's Seasons.* Davenport is a retired professor and lives in Kentucky.

Rita Dove (born 1952) is the current Poet Laureate of the United States and a Pulitzer Prize-winning author who has published five poetry collections, most recently *Selected Poems;* a novel, *Through the Ivory Gate;* and the verse drama *The Darker Face of the Earth.* Dove lives with her husband and daughter in Charlottesville, where she is Commonwealth Professor of English at the University of Virginia.

Jacques Dupin (born 1927) is a French poet who has also published major studies of Joan Miró and Alberto Giacometti and written extensively on many contemporary artists. He lives in Paris, where he is preparing a catalogue raisonné of the works of Joan Miró.

Stuart Dybek (born 1942) is the author of a book of poems and two books of short stories, the latest being *The Coast of Chicago.* He is a professor of English at Western Michigan University, Kalamazoo.

Reginald Gibbons (born 1947) has most recently published a book of poems entitled *Maybe It Was So* and a novel, *Sweetbitter.* He is the editor of *TriQuarterly* magazine at Northwestern University, Evanston, Illinois.

Jorie Graham (born 1951) is an American poet who was raised in Italy. Her most recent collections of verse include *Region of Unlikeness* and *Materialism.* She is currently teaching at the Writers' Workshop in Iowa.

Patricia Hampl (born 1946) has published several volumes of prose and poetry, including *A Romantic Education* and *Resort & Other Poems,* and most recently *Virgin Time.* She is a professor at the University of Minnesota.

Robert Hayden (1913–1980) was a poet and university professor. His books, including *Selected Poems* and *Angle of Ascent,* illuminated the African-American experience.

Shelby Hearon (born 1931) is the author of thirteen novels, including *Hug Dancing, Owning Jolene,* and, most recently, *Life Estates.* A recent visiting professor at the University of Illinois, Chicago, she currently teaches in the writing program of the University of Miami.

Edward Hirsch (born 1950) has published four books of poems: *For the Sleepwalkers, Wild Gratitude, The Night Parade,* and, most recently, *Earthly Measures.* He teaches at the University of Houston and has been poet-in-residence at The Art Institute of Chicago.

John Hollander (born 1929) has recently published *Tesserae* and *Selected Poetry. The Gazer's Spirit,* a critical study of poems that confront particular works of art, will be published by the University of Chicago Press in 1995. He teaches English at Yale University.

Miroslav Holub (born 1923) is a Czech immunologist and writer. His latest publications include a poetry collection, *Vanishing Lung Syndrome,* a collection of essays entitled *Dimension of the Present Moment,* and a scientific monograph, *Immunology of Nude Mice.*

Richard Howard (born 1929) is the author of ten volumes of verse, the most recent being *Like Most Revelations.* He is a critic and a translator of French literature and the poetry editor of *The Paris Review.* He teaches at the University of Houston.

Charles Johnson (born 1948) is the Pollock Professor of English at the University of Washington, Seattle, as well as a novelist, screenwriter, critic, cartoonist, and essayist. His novel *Middle Passage* won the 1990 National Book Award for fiction.

Stanley Kunitz (born 1905) is a Pulitzer Prize-winning author whose publications include *The Testing-Tree; Poems of Akhmatova; The Poems of Stanley Kunitz, 1928–1978; Next-to-Last Things;* and *Interviews and Encounters with Stanley Kunitz. Passing Through: New & Later Poems* will be published in 1995.

Li-Young Lee (born 1957) was born in Jakarta, Indonesia, and lives in Chicago. He has published two books of poetry—*Rose* and *The City in Which I Love You*—and is currently working on a memoir.

Philip Levine (born 1928), a native of Detroit, has won two National Book awards and will publish his sixteenth volume of poetry, *The Simple Truth*, in November 1994. His most recent book is *The Bread of Time: Toward an Autobiography*. He lives in California.

Mina Loy (1882–1966) was born in London and lived in Paris during the 1920s, later moving to the United States. She was associated with American poets of the Imagist movement, including Ezra Pound. Her poems have been collected in several volumes: *Lunar Baedeker; Lunar Baedeker and Time Tables: Selected Poems;* and *The Last Lunar Baedeker: The Poems of Mina Loy.*

Cynthia Macdonald (born 1928) is a psychoanalyst who is preparing a book on her work with patients who have writing blocks. Her most recent book is *Living Wills: New and Selected Poems.* She lives in Houston.

William Maxwell (born 1908) was born in Lincoln, Illinois, and later moved to Chicago. He has published six novels, three collections of short fiction—the most recent being *Billie Dyer and Other Stories*—a volume of essays and reviews, a family memoir, and a book for children. He was, for forty years, a fiction editor at *The New Yorker.* He lives in New York City.

Susan Mitchell (born 1944) is the author of two books of poems, *Rapture* and *The Water Inside the Water.* She is at work on a third book of poems and a collection of essays. She is a professor at Florida Atlantic University and lives in Boca Raton.

Joyce Carol Oates (born 1938) is a novelist, short-story writer, poet, and critic who won the National Book Award in 1970. The author of over twenty novels, as well as several volumes of short stories and poetry, she is currently the Roger S. Berlind Distinguished Professor in Humanities at Princeton University.

Francine Prose (born 1947) is the author of ten works of fiction, most recently a story collection, *The Peaceable Kingdom.* She lives in upstate New York.

Carl Sandburg (1878–1967) was the author of books of poetry, history, biography, fiction, and music. He established his career as part of the Chicago literary renaissance with the publication of *Chicago Poems* in 1916. Among his most important works is his six-volume study of the life of Abraham Lincoln.

Delmore Schwartz (1913–1966) was born in Brooklyn and lived in Manhattan. He was a poet, fiction writer, essayist, translator, and teacher who was widely acclaimed for his first book of poems, *In Dreams Begin Responsibilities.*

Charles Simic (born 1938) has published fifteen collections of poetry since 1967. He has written essays on modernist poetics and has translated contemporary Yugoslav poetry. His latest work is *Hotel Insomnia.* Simic teaches at the University of New Hampshire. He was awarded the Pulitzer Prize in 1990.

Susan Sontag (born 1933), a graduate of the University of Chicago, has most recently published a novel, *The Volcano Lover,* and a play, *Alice in Bed.* In 1990 she was awarded a five-year fellowship by the MacArthur Foundation. She is completing another novel.

Jon Stallworthy (born 1935) is an English poet, critic, translator, and biographer who has taught at Cornell University. He lives in Oxford, England.

Gerald Stern (born 1925) is the author of *Leaving Another Kingdom: Selected Poems* and *Bread Without Sugar.* He teaches at the Writers' Workshop in Iowa.

Wallace Stevens (1879–1955) was one of America's most respected poets. A master stylist of highly intellectual poetry, he also maintained a career as an insurance executive. Stevens won the Pulitzer Prize in 1955.

Susan Stewart (born 1952) is the author of two volumes of poetry, *Yellow Stars and Ice* and *The Hive;* and three volumes of literary and aesthetic theory, *Nonsense, On Longing,* and *Crimes of Writing.* She lives in Philadelphia.

Mark Strand (born 1934) is the author of eight volumes of poetry. The most recent is *Dark Harbor.* He lives in Baltimore and teaches in the writing seminars at Johns Hopkins University.

John Updike (born 1932), a native of Shillington, Pennsylvania, graduated from Harvard College in 1954 and subsequently studied for a year at the Ruskin School of Drawing and Fine Art in Oxford, England. His most recent book is a novel, *Brazil.* A collection of short fiction, *The Afterlife and Other Stories,* is to be published in the fall of 1994.

Ellen Bryant Voigt (born 1943) has published four volumes of poetry, including, most recently, *Two Trees.* She founded and directed the MFA Writing Program at Goddard College and teaches in its relocated incarnation at Warren Wilson College in Swannanoa, North Carolina. Voigt lives with her husband and two children in Vermont.

John Edgar Wideman (born 1941) is a novelist and short-story writer. His collections of stories, most set in Homewood, the African-American section of Pittsburgh where he was raised, include *Fever, Philadelphia Fire,* and his recent publication *All Stories Are True.*

Richard Wilbur (born 1921), a former Poet Laureate (1987), has most recently published *New and Collected Poems,* which received a Pulitzer Prize. His verse translations of French drama—seven plays by Molière and two by Racine—are widely performed in the English-speaking world. He and his wife live in Key West and northwestern Massachusetts.

C. K. Williams (born 1936) is the author of a number of collections of poetry, the most recent of which is *A Dream of Mind.* He has also completed several translations, including Euripides's *Bacchae,* and has written several plays. His *Selected Poems* will be published in 1994. He is a professor of English at George Mason University, Fairfax, Virginia.

Garry Wills (born 1934) teaches history at Northwestern University, Evanston, Illinois, and is the author of *Lincoln at Gettysburg,* which won a Pulitzer Prize, and, most recently, *Certain Trumpets: The Call of Leaders.*

Charles Wright (born 1935), a native of Tennessee, is the author of ten volumes of poetry, including his recent *The World of Ten Thousand Things.* An eleventh book, *Chickamauga,* is due in 1995. He lives in Virginia.

John Yau (born 1950) is a writer, critic, and curator whose recent publications include a book of poems, *Edificio Sayonara,* and two books of criticism, *In The Realm of Appearances: The Art of Andy Warhol* and *A. R. Penck.* A book of his short stories, *Hawaiian Cowboys,* will be published in 1994.

Adam Zagajewski (born 1945) has most recently published a book of poems, *Canvas.* He teaches at the University of Houston.

COPYRIGHTS